Instructional Design

A Plan for Unit and Course Development

SECOND EDITION

Jerrold E. Kemp, Ed.D.
Coordinator
Instructional Development Services
San José State University

Fearon Publishers, Inc.

Belmont, California

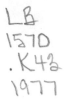

edited by Judith Quinn

designed by Rick Chafian

cover by Eleanor Mennick

Preface

In 1971, when the first edition of *Instructional Design* was published, people in the education field were just starting to give serious attention to the matter of systematic approaches to instructional planning. The bibliography in that edition listed just five references to other plans for designing instruction. In this edition the Bibliography includes twenty-nine. Psychologists, curriculum planners, and media specialists have all been active in developing and applying planning techniques of varying degrees of complexity.

The purpose of this book is to present a basic approach to systematic instructional planning that can be adapted for use on any educational or training level. It takes into consideration all major elements of the planning process, presenting the essential information about them in a straightforward, nontechnical manner.

My own experiences in using the book over the past several years, as well as feedback from others who have used it, have led to extensive revisions. For example, more attention is given here than in the previous edition to such topics as nonmeasurable objectives, individualized learning methods, the selection of media, and techniques for evaluating the learning of individual students and the effectiveness and efficiency of planned programs.

The book is intended to be useful to school administrators interested in encouraging their faculties to explore new methods of planning and instruction. It can be a step-by-step guide for individual teachers or for teaching teams, as they work out new courses or prepare to revise existing ones. Its content and organization can also be important to instructional developers or designers (roles increasingly being recognized in schools and colleges) as they work with teachers and planning teams.

The first edition has been used as the basis for college courses, workshops, and continuing-education programs, as well as by individuals studying on their own. This edition will find the same and, no doubt, additional uses. Even the study of instructional design *itself* is making use of the newer techniques described here!

The book is part of an instructional package prepared by the author which includes a detailed study guide and workbook with learner-participation activities for each chapter, and audio cassette recordings to guide and evaluate learning. (For further information about these materials, write Jerrold E. Kemp, Instructional Resources Center, San José State University, San José, California 95192).

Contents

APPENDIX

Part One

This book starts out by recognizing some of the important concerns and frustrations educators face today, allowing you to identify among them those matters you feel need your attention. Then the book presents the framework for developing improved instructional practices as a solution for many of them. This sets the stage for Parts 2 and 3.

A *Is This Book for You?*

Are you one of an increasing number of individuals in education who is disturbed by the inefficiency and ineffectiveness of traditional educational methods and by their results? Can we continue to ask for increased funding for education and yet not provide satisfactory answers to questions about whether the taxpaying public is getting its dollar's worth? More important, how do we recognize and better provide for the abilities, attitudes, and ambitions of our students, who reflect our rapidly changing society?

Specifically, do you ever ask yourself questions like the following?

- Why do students find much of the material they are assigned, to be irrelevant to them?
- Why are students often bored by the ways they are taught?
- How can *I* do a better job of serving the individual needs and interests of my students?
- What should be *my* role in improving instruction?
- Is there a better way to plan for effective instruction?
- Can education really be improved, within the limitations of available funds, personnel, and facilities?

Such questions are becoming increasingly important, but manageable solutions to them are slow in forthcoming. In speeches and in the professional literature there are many "we need to . . ." statements, but very few speakers and writers offer "how to . . ." suggestions for satisfactory solutions to educational problems.

Some years ago, Don Davies, then Associate Commissioner of Education in the United States Office of Education, listed ten directions in which he felt changes must take place in education:

3

1. To move *from* a mass approach to teaching and learning, *toward* more individualized diagnosis and teaching
2. To move *from* the traditional emphasis on reciting and listening, *toward* more participation and creative activity on the part of students
3. To move the school *from* its ivory tower aloofness, *toward* existence in and involvement in the total community and its problems
4. To move *from* negative attitudes toward youth who are different, *toward* a positive attitude of valuing and developing every pupil for his own unique potential
5. To move *from* a white middle-class orientation in curriculum and activities, *toward* a multicultural point of view that will build strength from diversity
6. To move *from* a fear of instructional technology, *toward* effective utilization of appropriate new media
7. To move *from* academic snobbism and prestige complexes, *toward* a recognition of many kinds of excellence
8. To move *from* the crystallization of meeting requirements and passing courses, *toward* evaluation that measures meaningful performance in life situations
9. To move *from* an educational system that seems to be run for the convenience and comfort of the administrator, *toward* a philosophy and practice that stimulates and encourages teacher creativity in solving educational problems
10. To move *from* the pattern of self-contained teachers presenting a self-contained curriculum in a self-contained classroom, *toward* flexible and differentiated approaches that utilize diversified talents of a teaching team in the most effective fashion[1]

The foregoing questions and statements require new ways of approaching instructional planning. If some of them concern you, then this book can assist you toward satisfying those concerns.

Getting Ready for Innovative Planning

Successful innovation in education requires at least three major elements: (1) teachers who are deeply concerned about their teaching effectiveness and who are motivated by a desire for improvement, (2) administrators who willingly encourage and support those teachers, and (3) a carefully designed plan for developing improved instructional practices. Of these three elements the

---

[1.]Unpublished memorandum, April 1969.

greatest shortcoming is often found in the third—the instructional design plan. Teachers and administrators may be ready to move forward, but too often a new plan is developed in terms of the traditional instructional approach. Although it may contain some new ideas, the framework of the plan is old. This can only perpetuate an outdated, impractical system. Regardless of the dedication and effort of individuals, the immediate success of such a plan is usually limited. In time, teaching practices return to their former level of ineffectiveness.

How can a single teacher, a teaching team, or a curriculum development group bring a fresh approach to planning or revising a unit of study? This book offers a plan for this, together with practical suggestions and realistic examples of how to proceed in order to achieve the learning outcomes now demanded of educational programs.

Students, teachers, and curriculum planners will find its content useful. But beyond these people, with established positions in education, are others who are filling a new role. They offer guidance and service to the teacher and to the planning team in developing all aspects of new programs. These professional educators are *instructional designers,* to whom this book, with its consideration of an instructional design plan and technological developments for improving education, should be of great interest.

B The Instructional Design Plan

In the past, plans for instruction and teaching have been made largely by intuition, and have often been based on ambiguous purposes and casual subjective judgments. The main concern has been with methods of teaching, rather than with learning—with the means rather than the outcomes of education.

It has become evident that the *instructional process* is complex—even more so than was formerly realized. It is composed of many interrelated parts and functions that must operate in a coherent manner in order to achieve success. By manipulating or controlling one or only a few of those parts or functions, we will not achieve the hoped-for success in improving the key outcome of education—learning by students. No matter how noble the intent or how well financed an instructional plan may be, a plan cannot bring about effective change if it attempts to impose new methods or new materials on the traditional school structure, the same routine, and the same personnel capabilities and attitudes.

Systems Approach and Instructional Technology

In order to intelligently relate all elements of the instructional process in building a successful program, an approach similar to one used widely in business, industry, the military, and space exploration is receiving increased attention. This method involves the development of an overall plan incorporating the interrelated parts of an instructional process in a sequential pattern. It is called the *systems approach* to problem-solving. The process is based on

6

the method of scientific inquiry, whereby a problem is recognized, a hypothesis is formed, experiments are conducted, and data are gathered from them that lead to a conclusion about the accuracy of the hypothesis. If it is correct, the results are used to produce or improve the products of technology. If not, new approaches are tried until success is realized.

When this procedure is applied to instructional planning, the term *instructional technology* is used. It means the systematic design of instruction, based on knowledge of the learning process and on communications theory, taking into consideration as many factors and variables of the particular situation as possible, so that successful learning will result.

For many people, the term *instructional technology* means the resources of instruction—machines (projectors, recorders, computers, and so on) and materials (films, slides, recordings, maps, and such). That is one meaning, but another, more important, understanding of the term is as the *process* of systematic planning that establishes a way to examine instructional problems and needs, sets a procedure for solving them, and then evaluates the results. It is this definition of instructional technology with which we are mainly concerned.

Engineers, psychologists, systems designers, and others from fields outside education have been the main forces in applying the systems concept to education. They often use technical jargon with impersonal, machinelike meanings and complex flow diagrams that imply an automated, robot-directed process. Largely because of this, the reactions of many educators to any application of the systems concept to instruction tends to be both negative and emotional because their superficial understanding of the method of technology equates it with machines only. Even educators interested in exploring this approach may find the complete systems method too involved and unmanageable for their purposes. To them, the procedures seem more appropriate to the narrow requirements of industrial job training than to the humanizing needs of academic education.

A method that focuses on learning outcomes, encompassing both the things we can specify and also those we can only anticipate, can become a realistic plan for designing improved instruction. It can build on the old, making use of familiar language. It can draw from valuable experience in such areas as programmed instruction (specification of objectives, presentation of subject matter in small steps, and continual evaluation of student learning) and techniques for producing audiovisual materials (primarily, production planning for motion pictures and television), and it can incorporate important elements from the systems approach. This is the type of straightforward plan proposed here.

The Instructional Design Plan

Let us call the approach and procedures described here an *instructional design*. This method can be applied on any educational level—elementary, secondary, or college. It can best be applied first to individual topics and then to units and then to complete courses, initially involving one or a few teachers. When the instructional designer and teachers have become fully familiar with the design plan, it may be applied to the efforts of an entire department or grade level.

This plan is designed to supply answers to three questions, which may be considered the *essential elements* of instructional technology:

1. What must be learned? *(objectives)*
2. What procedures and resources will work best to reach the desired learning levels? *(activities and resources)*
3. How will we know when the required learning has taken place? *(evaluation)*

The plan consists of eight parts:

1. Consider goals, and then list topics, stating the general purposes for teaching each topic.
2. Enumerate the important characteristics of the learners for whom the instruction is to be designed.
3. Specify the learning objectives to be achieved in terms of measurable student behavioral outcomes.
4. List the subject content that supports each objective.
5. Develop pre-assessments to determine the student's background and present level of knowledge about the topic.
6. Select teaching/learning activities and instructional resources that will treat the subject content so students will accomplish the objectives.
7. Coordinate such support services as budget, personnel, facilities, equipment, and schedules to carry out the instructional plan.

8. Evaluate students' learning in terms of their accomplishment of objectives, with a view to revising and reevaluating any phases of the plan that need improvement.

The diagram that follows illustrates the relationship of each step in the plan to the other steps.

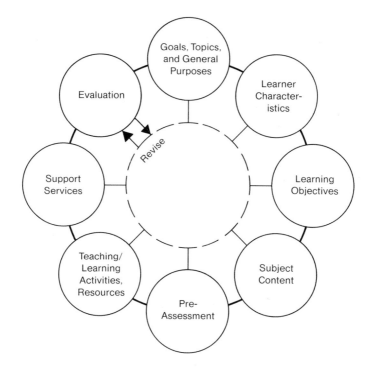

This is a flexible process. There is an interdependence among the eight elements; decisions relating to one may affect others. You can start with whichever element you are ready to start with and then move back and forth to the other steps. The sequence and order are your choice. Eventually, however, you should treat most of the eight. The plan is examined in detail in Part 2. The chapters present the elements in an order that might ideally be followed, but set your own pattern. The broken lines in the diagrams indicate revisions of elements made necessary by evaluation data gathered on students' accomplishment of objectives.

In some cases it may be possible to simplify or reorder phases of this plan and still improve learning. You must be the judge of such changes. But, first start with an examination of the total plan, as detailed here; then adapt it to your own needs and situations.

The remainder of this text discusses the following:

1. The details of the instructional design plan
2. A method for handling the mechanics of the planning process
3. The personnel capabilities required for planning and implementing the program
4. Techniques for working with teachers and support personnel to assure the success of the program
5. Ways to measure the effectiveness and efficiency of the plan
6. Suggestions you may find useful as you move ahead with your own applications of this plan

Part Two

Part 2 examines the steps of the instructional design plan and shows how each one can be developed in actual practice. Some steps are treated briefly because they are common procedures with which most educators are familiar. Other steps require more extensive explanation.

This book does *not* treat in detail such topics as the usual classroom methods or how to construct tests. Books on teaching methods handle these topics satisfactorily. When I suggest a new approach or a refinement, however, the text explores it in detail. On some topics I also refer you to other writers for related ideas and for deeper treatment. You are encouraged to examine these references and to have them at hand as you implement the plan proposed here in your own courses.

Although I consider the elements of the plan separately and in sequence, there is a close relationship among all steps, as explained in Chapter B. The order in which some steps occur is flexible. But, remember, what you plan for one step may affect what is done in another one. This also means that during your planning, ideas, facts, or examples may come to mind that have value at later stages. Be sure to write them down for future reference.

At the end of each chapter you will find examples selected from the five representative subject areas listed in Table 1, to illustrate the step of the instructional design plan that is discussed in that chapter.

Space permits only limited examples. Because it is difficult to perceive the continuity of treatment of any one example (since each element is listed pages apart from the next), the complete design plan for each subject, with all eight steps of the plan, also appears in the Appendix.

Table 1. Examples from Representative Subject Areas

Subject Area	Unit	Topic	Educational Level	Remarks
Example 1. language arts	literature of other countries	haiku	grade 8	• attention to attitudinal as well as knowledge objectives • group and independent work • integral use of media
Example 2. vocational guidance	building trades	sheet-metal craft	high school	• emphasis on individual learning • flexible use of resources • leads students to decision-making
Example 3. interdisciplinary (Social Studies and Physical Sciences)	contemporary problems	the future	grades 11 and 12	• primarily small-group activities • freedom for creative work • media used for communicating outcomes
Example 4. instructional technology	projected audio-visual materials and equipment	overhead projection	college (teachers education)	• individualized format • multiple resources for students to select and use
Example 5. allied health services	basic skills laboratory	technique for washing hands for medical asepsis	paraprofessional training	• complete individualized module

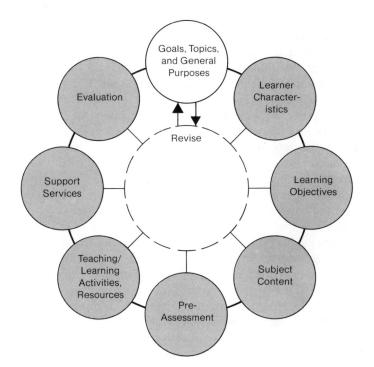

1 Goals, Topics, and General Purposes

What do you want to accomplish in teaching each topic?

Most often, instructional design planning starts with a recognition of the broad *goals* of the school system or institution. The educational program is then developed to serve those goals. Within curriculum areas or courses, *topics* are chosen for study, for each of which the teacher explicitly expresses the *general purposes* (what students generally are expected to learn as a result of instruction).

Identifying Goals

All educational programs are based on broadly stated goals. Those goals may be derived from three sources—society, students, subject areas. Societally determined goals include such broad concepts as "establishing personal values inherent in change," "developing responsibility and concern for self and others," and "selecting personal objectives but being open to alternatives." Such goals involve philosophical and ethical considerations derived from the perceived wishes or demands of the community, the nature of the institution, or other direction-establishing elements that control the particular educational program.

Students' educational goals may include "job preparedness," "problem-solving skills," or "constructive use of leisure time."

Goals related to subject areas may be stated more specifically in such terms as "to be aware of beauty and orderliness in the environment" (science), "to develop the ability to communicate effectively by oral or written means" (language arts), or "to stimulate an appreciation of the Spanish-American culture and thereby facilitate the study of the Spanish language" (foreign language). Such goals relate to broad competencies that will help learners to participate satisfactorily in society. They may also be the bases for the understandings and skills the society expects the institution to transmit. Statements of goals should recognize changes in learners' needs and interests, as well as changes in the needs of society and its institutions.

[Because of a need or desire to pay attention to student interests and needs, you may want to start your planning with a consideration of learner characteristics (Chapter 2). Then you could return to the selection of topics and general purposes, in terms of the nature of your students. The approach is flexible—arrange the planning steps in an order that is most suitable for you.]

Selecting Topics

After recognizing or establishing its goals, a planning team should list the *major topics* to be treated within the content area. Those topics, or unit headings, would become the scope of the course or program, the basis for the instruction. For a college course on meteorology such topics as "air masses," "weather fronts," "weather symbols," "weather maps," and "forecasting" might be selected. In a primary-grade program units might include "Living Things and Their Basic Needs," "Children Have Many Needs," and "Families Live in Communities."[1]

Often we start with high hopes of developing a new course or restructuring the content and instructional methods of a conventional program. But, it can be too easy to fall back on traditional topics, content, and methods.

Topics are usually sequenced according to a logical organization, most often from simple or concrete levels to complex and more abstract levels. Consideration should also be given to ordering topics so they build on knowledge and skills students have acquired in previous courses or at earlier stages in the course sequence. And sometimes people even organize topics according to their own subject preferences or teaching experiences.

Gradually the traditional academic divisions between subject areas are being reduced. Teachers from different disciplines, like English and art, or economics and biology, may work together in teams to plan interdisciplinary programs. The planning process you are starting to examine is particularly essential for handling the complexities of designing such interdisciplinary or problem-centered programs because of the numerous interrelated details that need consideration.

At this point it becomes necessary to decide how many topics should be treated and to what depth. You must consider such factors as how soon the program must be ready, the possibility of correlating the content with that of another course, and any restrictions set by learner characteristics and by the limitations of budget, facilities, resources, and personnel of the teaching institution.

Listing General Purposes

When teachers first write objectives, many of them use such terms as *"to understand* about a topic," *"to appreciate* a subject," *"to acquire* skill in an activity," or *"to become aware* of certain events." As you may already know—or as you will learn—such ambiguous words do not state precise learning objectives. Yet, they are important as an initial expression, signifying broadly what the teacher

---

[1]Adapted from *Man's Needs: A Sequential Kindergarten Social Studies Program* (San Diego: San Diego Unified School District, 1971).

wants to accomplish in the topic. They usually express the planners' *own aims or purposes* for the topic or unit.

At the outset of planning, it is unrealistic to ask a teacher or a team to state meaningful learning objectives. (This is a difficult task, as we shall see, which may even discourage enthusiasm for following a systematic planning procedure.) Therefore, accept a general statement of purpose as the starting point for your planning.

Some of the expressions commonly used to describe general purposes for a topic are listed below:

to acquire a skill	to comprehend	to learn
to appreciate	to determine	to like
to become aware of	to enjoy	to master
to become familiar with	to grasp the significance of	to perceive
to be introduced to	to have a feeling for	to understand
to believe in	to know	to use

You may eventually decide on setting several objectives to accomplish one broad, general purpose, just as you may use a single topic to serve more than one purpose. So, write down each general purpose. Then you can derive objectives that will serve as specific learning outcomes from them.

The decision to select one or more purposes to represent a topic to be taught is the responsibility of the teachers or the members of the teaching team. Their training and their knowledge of the subject content and of the student group qualify them—and only them—to make this selection. A professional instructional designer can help the teacher state the chosen purposes in clear, comprehensive fashion. But it is not the designer's responsibility to question what is to be taught. The designer's main contribution is to clarify the statements of purpose with the teacher and help the teacher translate them into detailed behavioral terms for which learning experiences can be planned.

So, planning for instruction often starts with teacher-oriented statements of general purposes for topics, selected in relation to the broad goals of an institution or program. General purposes for our sample topics might include the following.

HAIKU

To develop an appreciation for haiku by writing it.

SHEET-METAL CRAFT

To motivate an interest in the sheet-metal craft as a vocation

THE FUTURE

To help students consider the world of the future and its possible effects on their lives

OVERHEAD PROJECTION

To be prepared for using the overhead projector in teaching

TECHNIQUE FOR WASHING HANDS

1. To understand that the reason for washing hands is to maintain standards of cleanliness
2. To learn the correct technique for washing hands

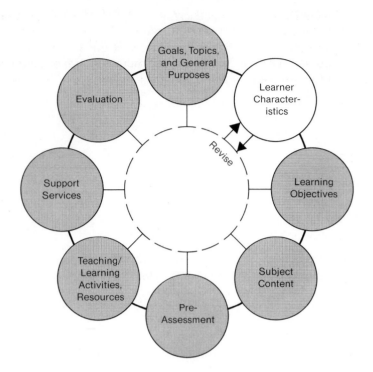

2 *Learner Characteristics*

*What factors do you want to know about the
student group or individual learners that
will affect plans for their learning?*

   To best assure an individual's success in his or her educational
program, we should recognize and respect the student as an individual learner. Ideally, each person should be assisted in pursuing
learning at his or her own pace, on his or her own schedule, and
with his or her own selection of learning experiences and materials.
To serve both group and individual means that we must obtain
information about the learners' capabilities, needs, and interests.
These should affect the emphases in instructional planning, including the selection of topics and the level at which topics are intro-

duced, the choice and sequencing of objectives, the depth of treatment, and the variety of learning activities.

When designing an instructional plan, you must very early decide for yourself which of the following characteristics of your students would be most helpful for you to know:

Academic factors: number of students; academic background; grade-point average; level of intelligence; reading level; scores on standardized achievement and aptitude tests; study habits; ability to work alone; background in the subject or topic; motivation for studying the subject; expectations of the course; vocational and cultural aspirations

Social factors: age; maturity; attention span; special talents; physical and emotional handicaps; relations among students; socioeconomic situation

Much of this information can be obtained from students' cumulative records and from consultations with other teachers, student counselors, and advisers. Results of questionnaires, as well as attitudinal surveys completed by students and pre-assessment tests (see Chapter 5), also can provide useful data for making planning decisions.

Other factors such as learning conditions and learning styles should be taken into account when planning, as well. These characteristics can become particularly important, of course, when you are developing an individualized learning program.

Learning Conditions

Learning conditions refer to groups of factors that can affect a person's ability to concentrate, absorb, and retain information.[1] We all know teenagers who can best study with popular music blasting at full volume from the radio. They feel comfortable with a noise background, ignoring it when they concentrate. How each person

---

[1.]Rita Dunn and Kenneth Dunn, *Educator's Self-Teaching Guide to Individualizing Instructional Programs* (West Nyack, N.Y.: Parker Publishing Co., 1975), pp. 74–93. I use the expression *learning conditions* to describe the methods employed by Dunn and Dunn in grouping and determining student characteristics. The term *learning styles,* which relates to certain of the Dunn and Dunn conditions, is the descriptor I employ in the following text.

responds to sound in the learning environment may be an important condition of that person's learning. Dunn and Dunn describe four conditions: the physical environment (sound, light, temperature, and choice and arrangement of furniture), the emotional environment (individual motivation, persistence in a task, and taking responsibility), the sociological environment (preference for individual or group work, response to an authority figure, and so on), and a student's own physiological makeup (sensory strengths and weaknesses, need for food, restlessness or need for mobility, daily use of time or biorhythm for efficient functioning). They have developed a detailed questionnaire that can help a teacher analyze the conditions under which a student is most likely to learn.[2]

Learning Styles

Some students find certain methods of learning more appealing and effective than others. Some profit more from a visual approach; others from verbal (listening and/or reading) experiences; and still others from physical activities and the manipulation of objects. The attempt to identify a person's unique learning styles relates to a procedure that has been receiving increasing attention. It is called *cognitive style mapping*.[3] This method provides a framework for describing and diagnosing each individual's way of searching for meaning when confronted with a particular educational task. Three sets of meaning-seeking behavior are examined.

The first set indicates to what extent a student tends to gather information by using any or all of the theoretical symbols (words and numbers), the five senses, and cultural codes (sources of subjective meaning). The second set indicates the influences a student brings to bear on deriving meaning from the information gathered via Set 1. (Does the student structure meaning in an individual fashion or primarily in terms of associates' perceptions or on the basis of the family's—or other authority's—ideas?) The third set

---

[2] Dunn and Dunn, *Self-Teaching Guide*, pp. 93–111.

[3] This explanation is adapted from "Educational Cognitive Style: A Key to Individualized Instruction," a presentation by Lee DeNike, Ralph Granger, Lee Mullally, and Seldon Strother at the annual convention of the Association for Educational Communications and Technology (AECT), Dallas, March 1975. (See Hill and Nunney, Bibliography, under "Learning Theory.")

indicates the manner in which the student reasons in deriving meaning—that is, how the student approaches a problem in the process of drawing a conclusion by analyzing, questioning, or otherwise appraising that which is under consideration. At the time of this writing, a fourth set, dealing with memory, is being developed.

In this technique the results of diagnostic tests and questionnaires are diagrammed as a map of the cognitive characteristics of an individual that can help the individual and the teacher select the most appropriate methods, materials, and experiences for that student.

This method may sound Orwellian—more in keeping with *1984*—but the more we can discover about how an individual can or prefers to learn, the more pleasant and effective that person's learning can be. As refinements in cognitive style mapping take place, we will be hearing more about it.

When planning for group instruction, obtain general indications of the academic and social characteristics of your students. This range of capabilities, interests, and needs can guide you in planning decisions for slow learners, average students, and superior achievers. For individualized learning, data on each student can aid in the selection of alternative activities and resources most appropriate for the student.

Learner characteristics that would be significant for the sample topics are listed below.

HAIKU

Average Grade 8 class, 35 students

IQ, 96–128

Reading levels, Grades 6–12

The topic of haiku was considered for class study after much interest was shown in a student's report on Japanese literature.

Students are capable of taking responsibility for independent projects. They enjoy sharing materials in small groups.

SHEET-METAL CRAFT

Any interested high school student

Generally below median socioeconomic background

IQ, range 95–112

Reading level, average or below grade

Most do not expect to go to college.

Some need challenges to keep them in school.

THE FUTURE

30 advanced students, Grades 11 and 12

In upper quartile intellectually

Reading ability, Grades 10–14

Mature enough to engage in inquiry experiences

The previous unit examined historical predictions about the present.

OVERHEAD PROJECTION

200 elementary teacher-education students

This unit is studied the semester before student teaching.

Some students have used the overhead projector a little; all have seen it used in classes.

Many profess having only limited mechanical ability.

TECHNIQUE FOR WASHING HANDS

60 first-year allied health professional trainees

Reading ability, Grades 8–14

Thirty-six students represent cultural minority groups.

High level of motivation

The previous topic gave background on microorganisms.

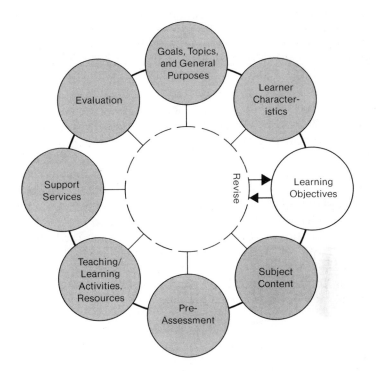

3 *Learning Objectives*

What should students know or be able to do,
or in what ways should they behave
differently, after studying this topic?

Our next step is the difficult but essential job of specifying learning objectives. We speak of *learning* objectives because our concern is with *learning* as the outcome of instruction. Learning requires active effort by the learner. Thus, all objectives must be stated in terms of activities that will best promote learning.

Good teachers have always told their students what performance and achievement levels were to be expected of them at test time. But now, primarily through what we have learned from the planning procedures for programmed instruction, we are more aware of the importance of indicating precise behavioral objectives

23

before we select learning activities. It is only by stating measurable objectives that we know specifically what it is that we want to teach and can later determine whether we have accomplished it.

Some instructional designers insist that objectives be stated carefully early in the planning—right after the goals or the statements of general purposes are formulated for a topic. Sequentially this may be correct, but in actual practice it does not always work. Many people cannot enumerate detailed objectives at that point because their own thinking about what to include in the unit may not be clear.

Writing objectives is a developmental activity that requires refinements, changes, and additions as the writer develops subsequent planning steps. For some teachers, objectives become evident only after subject content is outlined. Sometimes it is not until learning activities are being selected or evaluation methods stated that the "real" objectives for a topic become clear. Therefore, expect to start with loosely worded objectives, move ahead in the planning sequence, and then return to spell out the objectives in detail as each one becomes more evident.[1]

Categories of Objectives

Objectives for learning can be grouped into three major categories—*cognitive, psychomotor,* and *affective.* These areas (or *domains,* as they are generally called), are widely referred to in the literature that discusses objectives. Your understanding of the levels within each domain will help you to give attention to the higher levels of learning and behavior. Let's examine them.

The domain we give most attention to in educational programs is the *cognitive domain.* It includes objectives concerning knowledge, or information, and thinking—naming, recognizing, predicting, and so on. Benjamin S. Bloom and his associates have developed a taxonomy for the cognitive domain.[2] (A taxonomy is a method of sequential classification in progressively higher levels.) In this in-

---

[1] Robert F. Mager very capably makes the case for objectives in an instructional program. If you are not familiar with his brief, fascinating book *Preparing Instructional Objectives* (Belmont, Calif: Fearon Publishers, Inc., 1975), be sure to read it.

[2] Benjamin S. Bloom and others, *Cognitive Domain,* Taxonomy of Educational Objectives, Handbook 1 (New York: David McKay, 1956).

stance, it proceeds from simple knowledge to higher levels of mental activity:

1. KNOWLEDGE   ability to memorize, recall, or otherwise repeat information presented earlier
   Example   List the five main parts of a 35 mm camera.
2. COMPREHENSION   ability to interpret or restate the information acquired on Level 1 in one's own terms
   Example   Describe the sequence of six steps for loading film into a 35 mm camera.
3. APPLICATION   ability to use or apply information, theories, principles, or laws to new situations
   Example   Choose the three camera exposure settings for various picture-taking situations.
4. ANALYSIS   ability to divide complex knowledge into its separate parts and to recognize the relationship of those parts
   Example   Compare the way each camera setting is made on two different models of 35 mm camera.
5. SYNTHESIS   ability to bring together separate elements of knowledge to form new patterns or wholes
   Example   Plan a series of six subjects for a photographic slide sequence.
6. EVALUATION   ability to make judgments or appraisals based on knowledge or given criteria
   Example   Evaluate the quality of slides prepared by members of the class on a four-point rating scale.

The headings for this taxonomy flow from simple to more complex intellectual behaviors and from concrete to more abstract mental levels. Previously I mentioned that most attention in schools is given to this cognitive area. Within the domain, much schoolwork centers around Level 1—remembering information. One of the challenges in instructional planning is to devise learning objectives and activities that can help students have experiences on the five higher intellectual levels. Shortly, when we examine both the verbs used in expressing objectives and the sequencing of objectives, we will give further attention to all six levels.

The second category in which learning objectives may be grouped is the *psychomotor domain*. It treats the skills requiring use and coordination of skeletal muscles, as in the physical activities of performing, manipulating, and constructing. Although no widely accepted taxonomy of the psychomotor domain has been de-

veloped, various individuals have suggested such scales. One recognized grouping (although it is not a sequential taxonomy) is the
following:

1. GROSS BODILY MOVEMENTS   arms, shoulders, feet, and legs
   Examples   throwing a ball for a distance, picking up a heavy
   object so as not to strain oneself, performing a back dive
2. FINELY COORDINATED MOVEMENTS   hand and fingers; hand
   and eye; hand and ear; hand, eye, and foot
   Examples   knitting a scarf, guiding wood through a circular
   saw, typewriting, driving a car, sight-reading music while
   playing the organ
3. NONVERBAL COMMUNICATION   facial expression, gestures,
   bodily movements
   Examples   showing emotions through facial expressions,
   employing gestures to communicate directions, pantomiming
   a message
4. SPEECH BEHAVIOR   producing and projecting sound, coordinating sound and gestures
   Examples   giving instructions in a foreign language or presenting a literary reading, with gestures for emphasis[3]

From this list of psychomotor behaviors you can classify physical
skills relating to athletics, the performing arts, the manipulation of
tools, the operation of machines and other equipment, speaking,
and writing. Psychomotor behaviors generally are easy to observe,
describe, and measure. Task analysis (page 46) permits you to dif-
ferentiate the specific muscle coordination required in each such
physical activity and then state the appropriate learning requirements as objectives.

The third category of objectives is the *affective domain*. This involves objectives concerning attitudes, appreciations, values, and
all emotions—enjoying, conserving, respecting, and so on. We talk
about this area as being of great importance in education, but it is
the one with which we have been able to do the least—particularly
in writing useful learning objectives. David R. Krathwohl and his
associates have organized the affective domain into five levels.[4]

---

[3] Robert J. Kibler and others, *Behavioral Objectives and Instruction* (Boston: Allyn &
Bacon, 1970) pp. 66–75.

[4] David R. Krathwohl and others, *Affective Domain*, Taxonomy of Educational Objectives, Handbook 2 (New York: David McKay, 1964).

1. RECEIVING willing to give attention to an event or activity
   Example A student listens attentively to an announcement of a forthcoming meeting for the formation of an ecology-action group.
2. RESPONDING willing to react to an event through some form of participation
   Example The student attends the ecology-action group meeting.
3. VALUING willing to accept an event through the expression of a positive attitude
   Example The student helps the group formulate plans and draw up a list of activities in which to engage.
4. ORGANIZING when encountering situations to which more than one value applies, willingly organizes the values, determines the interrelationships, and accepts some as dominant (more important to the student)
   Example When the next meeting of the group is scheduled, the student decides to attend, rather than viewing a television program that interests the student or attending a school athletic event.
5. CHARACTERIZING BY A VALUE COMPLEX consistently acts in accordance with values the student accepts and incorporates this behavior as a part of his or her personality
   Example The student continues an active participation in the ecology-action group program for many years.

The levels of the affective domain, like those of the cognitive domain, form a continuum for attitudinal behavior, from simple awareness and acceptance to internalization, as attitudes become part of an individual's practicing value system. The problem of translating these feelings into identifiable and observable behavior makes the writing of attitudinal objectives very difficult. This matter receives more attention later, under the heading "Benefits and Limitations of Objectives."

Even though we have examined the three domains separately, you should recognize that they are closely related in two ways. First, a single objective can involve learning in two or more domains. For example, when an art student learns to mix colors, the student must acquire cognitive knowledge about colors and their relationships, as well as the psychomotor skills of handling the brush while mixing.

Second, attitudinal development may precede successful learning in the other domains. It is often necessary to motivate students to learn subject matter before successful instruction in that subject content can take place. This may be particularly true in an individualized learning program, since the student must take responsibility for his or her own learning and both receptiveness and cooperation can, in some measure, determine the student's level of achievement. On the other hand, a well-organized program in which the student participates successfully usually produces positive attitudes in the student toward the subject area and the instructor.

During planning, keep in mind all three domains, and attempt to treat the higher levels, as appropriate for your topics and general purposes. (Domains receive further attention later in this chapter.)

Difficulties in Writing Objectives

One reason many people shy away from stating precise objectives is that formulating them demands hard mental effort. Each objective—to the degree possible—should be unambiguous. It must mean exactly the same thing to all other teachers, and it must also clearly communicate to all students who will use it. Many teachers are not accustomed to such exactness in instructional planning. For too long we have based our teaching on broad generalizations, often leaving it up to the student to interpret what we actually mean.

It is not until the importance of objectives to an instructional program becomes apparent that teachers are willing to put sincere effort into preparing them. Then the difficulties and frustrations are taken in stride and teachers gradually develop a habit and pattern for expressing as many of the desired outcomes of student learning as possible in specific, unambiguous terms.

Writing Procedure

A learning objective is a precise statement that answers the question, "What does the student have to do in order to show that he or she has learned what you want the student to learn?" Ask yourself this question each time you start to formulate an objective. It will help give direction to your efforts. To answer the question satisfactorily, write objectives that consist of at least *two* essential parts and two optional parts; as follows:

1. Start with an *action verb* that describes a specific behavior or activity by the learner:

   > *name*   *make*   *arrange*   *compare*

2. Follow the action verb with the *content reference* that describes the subject being treated:

   > Name the fifty *state capitals.*
   > Make a 3' × 4' *doghouse.*
   > Arrange the *six steps in water purification.*
   > Compare the *cultures of two past civilizations.*

3. If the aforementioned essential parts of an objective lend themselves to some quantification, add a *performance standard* that indicates the minimum acceptable accomplishment in *measurable terms:*

   > Name the fifty state capitals with *an accuracy of 90 percent.*
   >
   > Make a 3' × 4' doghouse in *four hours according to the plans provided.*
   >
   > Arrange the six steps in water purification *in correct order.*
   >
   > Compare the cultures of two past civilizations, *enumerating at least five characteristics of each.*

   For a competency-based program, including such performance standards is almost essential for determining when a student reaches the satisfactory level of achievement.

4. As necessary for student understanding and in order to set evaluation requirements, add any *criteria* or *conditions* under which the learning must take place:

   > *As a team activity,* name the fifty state capitals with an accuracy of 90 percent.
   >
   > Make a 3' × 4' doghouse in four hours according to the plans provided, *using only the tools in your kit.*
   >
   > *When given a set of photographs,* arrange the six steps in water purification in correct order.
   >
   > *As based on the assigned readings,* compare the cultures of two past civilizations, enumerating at least five characteristics of each.

All learning objectives should be written in forms similar to those of the examples above. Where appropriate, include either or both of the optional parts (3 and 4). When no performance standard is included, the assumption is usually made that only a 100 percent correct reply is acceptable. Keep your statements simple and brief. Avoid including too much detail, so the effort of writing the objectives does not become discouraging to you and the requirements, overwhelming to your students.

A caution—when instructional planners first start to write objectives, they tend to write descriptions of what is to occur during the instruction as if they were learning objectives—for example, "to view a filmstrip on animal habitats" or "to read pages 45–60 in the text." But those are *activities*, not indications of learning outcomes. If you are not sure whether what you are stating is an objective, ask yourself, "Is this what I want the student to be able to do at the end of the topic or unit?"

Selecting the Action Verb

No doubt, you or other members of your planning team can easily choose the content reference for an objective. You also will have little difficulty in deciding on the standard of performance you want students to reach and the conditions under which learning is to take place. The selection of the appropriate action verb to describe the required student behavior is the difficult part of objective writing.

As indicated previously, most learning objectives in education programs are in the cognitive domain. Verbs that express behaviors on each of the six levels in Bloom's taxonomy are listed on page 31. They can help you recognize (and give attention to) the higher intellectual levels in your planning.

Levels of Objectives

The three domains often overlap, and an objective may require that the learner gain competence in more than a single element of knowledge or skill. Recall the example of the art student learning to mix colors. This requires knowledge about colors and skill in using the brush. Frequently, accomplishing the *major* learning objective is dependent on one or more other objectives.

Verbs Applicable to the Levels in the Cognitive Domain (Note: Depending on the use, some verbs may apply to more than one level.)

1. Knowledge

arrange	order
define	recognize
duplicate	relate
label	recall
list	repeat
memorize	reproduce
name	

2. Comprehension

classify	locate
describe	recognize
discuss	report
explain	restate
express	review
identify	select
indicate	tell
	translate

3. Application

apply	operate
choose	practice
demonstrate	schedule
dramatize	sketch
employ	solve
illustrate	use
interpret	

4. Analysis

analyze	differentiate
appraise	discriminate
calculate	distinguish
categorize	examine
compare	experiment
contrast	inventory
criticize	question
diagram	test

5. Synthesis

arrange	formulate
assemble	manage
collect	organize
compose	plan
construct	prepare
create	propose
design	set up
	write

6. Evaluation

appraise	judge
argue	predict
assess	rate
attach	score
choose	select
compare	support
defend	value
estimate	evaluate

A major objective is called a *terminal objective*. It describes in behavioral terms the major learning outcomes expressed originally as the general purpose. (More than one terminal objective may be necessary for accomplishing a single general purpose.)

The subobjectives that lead to accomplishing the terminal objective are designated *enabling, subordinate,* or *supportive objectives*. Supportive objectives describe the specific behaviors (single activities or steps) that must be learned or performed in order to achieve the terminal objective.

For example, under the topic "weather," a terminal objective may be "to interpret weather patterns shown on a weather map." Leading to it might be such supportive objectives as "to relate symbols used on a weather map to actual weather conditions" and "to recognize types of air masses, and their characteristics, as inferred on a map." Thus, the final, or terminal, objective is a complex learning task built upon a number of subordinate objectives.

As you list subject content or do a task analysis of your topic (page 46), the relationship of major items and supportive content becomes evident in outline form. You may find the subject content step to be a good starting point for developing your terminal and subordinate learning objectives.

Sequencing Objectives

By now, it should be evident that a number of methods for sequencing or classifying objectives according to levels of behavior have been developed. Levels of objectives is one sequencing procedure. Other important ones are found in the cognitive and affective domains, each of which includes a hierarchy (a classification sequence) starting from low levels of learning or behavior and progressing through more advanced or sophisticated levels. At this point you may wish to review the examples given for the six cognitive domains and the five affective domains on pages 25 and 27.

Another useful sequencing pattern for cognitive learning has been developed by psychologist Robert M. Gagné. He distinguishes eight types of learning and presents them as a hierarchy of knowledge and mental behaviors. The higher four levels relate to school-type learning experiences:

   a. FACTUAL LEARNING.   Items of information like names, dates, places, or events, which provide the basic terminology relating to a topic

b. CONCEPTUAL LEARNING. Discriminating among objects and events by classifying or grouping those that have similar characteristics under a general name

c. PRINCIPLE LEARNING. Statements that show the relationship among two or more concepts

d. PROBLEM-SOLVING. Applying principles to new situations by solving problems, explaining circumstances, inferring causes or effects, or predicting outcomes[5]

Each higher learning level is dependent upon the learner's having mastered the related lower-level learnings. Thus, a student uses *facts* to identify *concepts,* then builds relationships among concepts to identify *principles,* and ultimately applies principles to develop *problem-solving* skills. (See Chapter 4, "Subject Content," for further consideration of these four levels of learning behavior.)

Some relationship can be found between the categories of behavior that Gagné proposes and the taxonomy of objectives listed by Bloom in the cognitive area. They both start with simple factual learning and move to higher intellectual levels, and both include, according to each writer's interpretation, the important mental processes that are essential to learning.

Gagné explains which conditions are most appropriate for facilitating the learning of each type of performance. This method helps the planner answer these questions: "In order to be able to do or to understand this *concept* (principle, or whatever), what must the learner first be able to do, know, or understand?" Then, "Have I provided for this lower level of behavior?" Both Bloom's and Gagné's materials suggest systematic ways of grouping and sequencing objectives within a topic.

One challenge in designing a good instructional plan is to recognize the sequential levels of your topic and to realize that for many topics students should accomplish higher-order learning behaviors in one or more categories of objectives (cognitive, psychomotor, and affective). You then must devise measurable ways of assuring that such objectives are attained. (If you do not treat these more complex and abstract objectives, you are in danger of omitting them and following the easiest path by limiting objectives to the learning levels of memorization and factual recall, which may be overall of less importance.)

[5.]List adapted from Robert M. Gagné, *The Conditions of Learning* (New York: Holt, Rinehart and Winston Inc., 1970).

One way to check that a unit includes higher-level objectives is to prepare a specification table relating objectives to behaviors (Table 2). List the objectives vertically, and show which categories of behaviors they are in horizontally. From left to right move to increasingly abstract levels—as "learning facts," "forming concepts," "learning principles," and "problem-solving." (You may prefer other headings, like those of the cognitive or affective taxonomies.)

In preparing such a table, you will find that an objective does not always fall neatly into a single behavioral category. An objective you classify as "learning principles" might also seem to belong under "forming concepts." In this case, use the definitions of these terms, as expressed above. When a question of placement is still unresolved, place the objective under the higher level.

By preparing a table and then studying the relationships between objectives and behavior levels, you will be able to determine whether you are sequencing your objectives logically—that is, from simple to advanced levels.

Benefits and Limitations of Objectives

We are discussing a plan for systematic instructional planning in which the specification of learning objectives plays a key role. Obviously, therefore, I am in favor of developing objectives for instructional programs. What are some of the essential benefits of doing this?

- Objectives form the framework for any instructional program built on a competency base, where student mastery of learning is the hoped-for outcome.

- Objectives inform students what will be required of them. By knowing what to expect, students can better prepare their work. (Further attention is given to students and their objectives later in this chapter.)

- Objectives help the planning team to think in specific terms, and to organize and sequence the subject matter.

- Objectives indicate the type and extent of activities that are required for successfully carrying out the learning.

- Objectives provide a basis for evaluating both the student's learning and the effectiveness of the instructional program.

Table 2. A Specification Table Relating Objectives to
Cognitive Learning Levels

Objective	Learning Facts	Forming Concepts	Learning Principles	Problem-Solving
1. Name the common plane geometric figures.	●			
2. Define the common plane geometric figures.	●			
3. Identify geometric figures shown in pictures.		●		
4. Group similar geometric figures when shown models of various sizes.			●	
5. List dimensions of geometric figures.	●			
6. Label significant dimensions of geometric figures.		●		
7. Measure dimensions in sketches of geometric figures.				●
8. Make scale drawings of common geometric figures.				●
9. Derive the formulas for areas of geometric figures.			●	
10. Compute areas of geometric figures in diagrams.				●
11. Compare sizes of geometric figures in diagrams.			●	
12. Calculate areas of common objects.				●

• Objectives provide the best means for communicating to your colleagues, parents, and others what is to be taught and learned.

Let us also recognize some of the major limitations of learning objectives, as identified by those who do not believe they should be explicitly stated:

- Most objectives relate to the lowest cognitive level (recall of information); they are the least important, so the really important outcomes of education receive little attention.
- The procedure employed for specifying objectives applies best to cognitive and psychomotor behaviors. Only rarely can objectives in the affective domain be stated in observable and measurable terms.
- While objectives may be somewhat useful in subject areas that have a high sequential content structure, like mathematics, natural sciences, and foreign languages, they are of limited use in the humanities, arts, and social sciences, which do not require a sequential cognitive organization.
- A teacher cannot specify in advance all potential outcomes of an instructional program. Unanticipated needs and activities may lead to worthwhile results that might be missed if the narrow path of an objective-based program were followed rigidly.
- Employing measurable objectives is a dehumanizing approach to learning and makes education too mechanistic and impersonal.

These are some of the pros and cons about learning objectives. It isn't an either/or situation. The limitations to specifying objectives should be recognized, but there are ways of partially overcoming those shortcomings.

Admittedly, most objectives relate to short-term goals, attainable in one semester or one school year. Some of them, however, may contribute to long-term goals, such as the development of research, analytical, or decision-making abilities, over which the teacher has little or no control. These high-level objectives may not be fully measurable until years later in schooling or until the individual becomes an active member of society and is in a profession or vocation. Therefore, it is reasonable at times to assume that some objectives cannot be completely satisfied during the planned instructional program.

But, the great majority of desired instructional outcomes can be measured on an appropriate mastery level in a reasonable period of time. Even for those objectives that may be considered to be beyond immediate complete measurement, there still can be some standards against which a teacher can make a partial or intermediate judgment of the student's accomplishments.

Affective-Domain Objectives

When we turn to the affective area—attitudes and apprecia-tions—we do find it more difficult to specify objectives in clearly observable and measurable terms. Some behaviors in this area are hard to identify, let alone to name and measure. How, for instance, do you measure an attitude toward *becoming a good citizen* or an *appreciation of poetry*? This must be done indirectly from secondary clues. For example, to measure good citizenship, observe how the student treats other members of the class. Find out if the student participates actively in student government or shows other mani-festations of practicing the democratic process. For appreciating poetry, find out if the student voluntarily takes poetry books from the library. Does the student ever write poetry when given an op-tional assignment in English class?

Admittedly, these are only indications of the possible successful fulfillment of an attitudinal objective and do not measure it di-rectly. Mager calls these "approach tendencies" toward exhibiting a positive attitude to the subject or situation. The student's attitude is considered negative if he or she shows "avoidance tendencies."[6] In general terms, to measure an approach tendency toward a posi-tive attitude about an activity, you could use such indications as the following:

The student says he or she likes the activity.

The student selects the activity in place of other possible activ-ities.

The student participates in the activity with great enthusiasm.

The student shares his or her interest in the activity by discuss-ing it with others or by encouraging others to participate.

Some action verbs related particularly to the affective area are:

accepts	defends	judges	questions	visits
attempts	disputes	offers	shares	volunteers
challenges	joins	praises	supports	

---

[6]For further suggestions on formulating objectives in the affective area and for selecting measurable indicators of successful accomplishment, see another book by Robert F. Mager, *Developing Attitude Toward Learning* (Belmont, Calif.: Fearon Pub-lishers, Inc., 1969). Others are offered in *Behavioral Objectives in the Affective Domain*, National Science Supervisors Association, National Science Teachers Association, 1201 Sixteenth Street, N.W., Washington, D.C. 20036.

In *Goal Analysis* Mager helps us further to examine attitudinal goals we might select and then to specify indicator behaviors that represent positive actions relating to those attitudes.[7] For example, Mager suggests, if company employees are to exhibit *safety consciousness*, they can be expected to exhibit the following behavior: "report safety hazards; wear safety equipment; follow safety rules; practice good housekeeping (keep the work area free of dirt, grease, and tools); encourage safe practice in others (remind others to wear safety equipment); and so forth. . . ."

This is like the terminal/subordinate relationship of objectives. You might even do a task analysis of a general purpose in the affective domain! The method Mager suggests can help you to refine ways of indicating and then measuring attitudinal objectives.

But, realistically, there are many important objectives that cannot result in measurable outcomes. Elliott W. Eisner uses the term *expressive objectives*, for those for which specific outcomes cannot readily be stated.[8] Those objectives identify situations for the student, but they do not specify measurable outcomes. An expressive objective may allow for self-discovery, originality, and inventiveness. The result may be a surprise to both the student and the teacher. For example, "to develop a feeling of personal adequacy in athletic performance" is an expressive objective. By stating such nonmeasurable objectives during planning, you can at least identify aspects of educational goals that have personal or social importance and thus can make a start on deciding how to achieve them.

You should be aware that in any program there may be times when objectives need modification as the unit or course proceeds. You may have misjudged student preparation and readiness for pursuing an objective, or during discussion or study you may discover a new area of importance that should be investigated. In either case, be flexible. Revise an objective or add one, as student needs indicate.

[7.]Robert F. Mager, *Goal Analysis* (Belmont, Calif.: Fearon Publishers, Inc., 1972), p. 46.

[8.]Elliot W. Eisner, "Instructional and Expressive Objectives: Their Formulation and Use in Curriculum," in *Instructional Objectives: An Analysis of Emerging Issues,* W. James Popham, ed. (Chicago: Rand McNally, 1969) pp. 13–18.

Getting Help with Objectives

Should individual teachers or teaching teams formulate their own sets of objectives, even if objectives for that subject have already been developed by other teachers? Possibly not. Because developing useful objectives is difficult and time-consuming, wherever they can, teachers should obtain lists of already-formulated objectives, from which they can choose or adapt those that meet their needs. Or they can also use such lists just to get ideas for developing their own objectives.

Four sources from which you can obtain collections of objectives are listed below. (Any that are no longer available from their sources can be found in the reference resources of many school professional library collections.)

Directory of Measurable Objectives Sources (DIMOS). Director of Research, Educational Commission of the States, 1860 Lincoln St., Suite 822, Denver, Colo. 80203

Instructional Objectives: A National Compendium. State of Florida, Department of Education, Tallahassee, Fla. 32304

Instructional Objectives Exchange (IOX), Box 24095, Los Angeles, Calif. 90024

Selected Objectives for the English Language Arts, grades 7–12, by A. L. Lazarus and R. Knudson. Boston: Houghton Mifflin Company, 1967

Many books have been written about how to prepare objectives for instruction (see Bibliography). They present detailed treatments of objective-writing procedures and offer many practical suggestions beyond those included here.

Students and Their Objectives

At some time in the future mature students may decide on their own—or they will share the undertaking with teachers—what they will learn, instead of having it all done for them by teachers and curriculum planners.

Even today, there are experimental projects in which students are given a list of alternative objectives, from which each one decides individually which objectives to work on and in what order. This approach generally requires the use of a computer, with its almost limitless flexibility, to handle any order of choices and also to advise students whether, in the light of their backgrounds and pre-assessments, any selected objectives should be altered for successful learning.

You can begin to move in this direction of developing students' independence and responsibility, by informing your learners of the objectives they are to pursue. Such knowledge is instructive and also motivational. Objectives tell students:

- What goals they must attain
- What ideas and skills will be included in the upcoming instruction
- What types of behavior will be expected during evaluation

Present the objectives to students just as you have written them, including the performance criteria for success. "By the end of this unit you will be able to list . . . make . . . analyze . . . ." Thus, students know specifically what is expected of them and against what standard they will be evaluated.

Then justify your objectives. Many teachers assume that their choice of objectives will be accepted unquestioningly by students as necessary and worthwhile. This is not true. Students often question the merits of much of what they are directed to study. We owe it to them to tell *why* it is important for them to study a particular objective or group of objectives. Unless you can state an acceptable reason for including an objective, explaining how it is related to your general purposes, the objective may be trivial and unnecessary.

Albert A. Canfield recommends that when we give students a statement of objectives, we should include a secondary statement of rationale or justification explaining why each objective should be of importance to the learner. Thus students will understand better why they should study the content that supports the objective and where it fits within the topic. This procedure may not be necessary when the reason is obvious or when we can assume that an objective will have overwhelming student acceptance. But for many terminal objectives in a learning sequence the statement of justification has real value.[9]

---

[9]·Albert A. Canfield, "A Rationale for Performance Objectives," *Audiovisual Instruction* February 1968, pp. 127–129.

These two procedures—informing students of their objectives and justifying the objectives that need it—can bring about greater student cooperation. Students will know that you are helping them to set their paths for learning, and they will appreciate it.

In formulating a statement of justification, you may become more aware of the importance of an objective (or the lack of it) to the purpose of a topic or a unit. The justification will also direct you about how much or how little to emphasize an objective when you develop future learning experiences. This procedure can also serve as a check on the logical sequencing of your objectives.

The key points about objectives presented in this chapter are as follows:

- They indicate specifically what students are required to learn.
- They are classed in cognitive, psychomotor, or affective domains.
- They consist of an action verb and a content reference; and they may include performance standards and/or conditions.
- They can be categorized according to various levels of learning.
- They are more difficult to specify in the higher intellectual levels and in the affective area.
- They have both benefits and limitations that must be considered during planning.
- Nonmeasurable forms are recognized and should be stated.
- They may need to be modified or redeveloped as planning proceeds.
- Collections of objectives are available to teachers.
- Those designed for particular courses or units should be made available to students, together with a statement of justification for each.

Learning objectives for our sample topics are suggested below:

HAIKU

1. To describe the history and form of haiku, with reference to at least three other forms of Japanese poetry and three historical poets
   Justification: This will provide you with a background for understanding and appreciating this form of poetry.
2. To apply the three elements commonly used for description in haiku by writing a haiku on two pictorial subjects, each of which is rated at least "good" by a majority of the class on a scale. *(terminal objective)*
   Justification: The best way to learn about haiku is to write some yourself.
3. To express interest in haiku as a form of literature *(terminal objective)*
   Justification: This will indicate your appreciation of haiku.

SHEET-METAL CRAFT

1. To acquire information about the sheet-metal craft as a possible vocational choice *(terminal objective)*
   Justification: In order to examine this trade, you need the information that you can learn from achieving the following objectives.
   a. To describe four kinds of work done by sheet-metal craftspeople
   b. To identify five types of job opportunities and at least three employment advantages in the craft
   c. To list all educational courses and training required for entering the craft
2. To compare your interest in the sheet-metal craft with your interest in other crafts *(terminal objective)*
   Justification: With the information you have learned, you can make some assessment of your interest in and qualifications for this craft.

THE FUTURE

1. Identify what significant people are writing about the future.
2. Describe how those people arrived at their opinions.
3. Select one social or scientific area, and predict in detail how it will change or develop by the year 2000, and then describe the possible effects of the change upon you as an individual. *(terminal objective)*
   Justification: After examining what specialists say about the future, you should be able to make an educated guess about one aspect of the future and its influence on your life.

OVERHEAD PROJECTION

1. To operate the overhead projector with a rating of at least 9 on a 10-point scale *(terminal objective)*
   a. To set the projector in proper position for use
   b. To locate the three main controls
   c. To project three kinds of transparencies
   Justification: You must work with the projector yourself in order to understand its operation and gain confidence in using it.

2. To evaluate six transparencies you have selected, by completing an evaluation form for each one *(terminal objective)*
   a. To develop a rating scale for evaluating transparencies
   b. To use at least three sources in selecting your transparencies
   Justification: You will probably use many transparencies in your teaching. Therefore, you need a basis for judging their suitability and quality. This procedure will also help you establish a standard of quality for transparencies that you prepare for yourself.
3. To prepare three types of transparencies that, when projected, receive a rating of at least "good" from members of your class
   a. To make a transparency on acetate with felt pen
   b. To make a transparency using the thermal process
   c. To make a transparency using the diazo process
   Justification: You will need to learn to make your own transparencies because some subject content can be best presented that way.

TECHNIQUE FOR WASHING HANDS

1. Recognize why washing hands is essential for eliminating microorganisms in health-care work *(terminal objective)*
   Justification: You know the effects of microorganisms, and it is important that you also know the sources of microorganisms, so you can eliminate them.
   a. Name the four routes by which bacteria can be transmitted in a health-care facility
   b. State at least three circumstances under which you should wash your hands when working in a health-care facility.
2. Demonstrate proper hand-washing technique to two other students and the instructor with 100 percent proficiency *(terminal objective)*
   Justification: You must perform the skill to show your ability.
   a. Wash your hands without any contamination of hands, body, or clothing, performing the six necessary actions and requiring at least two minutes of time.

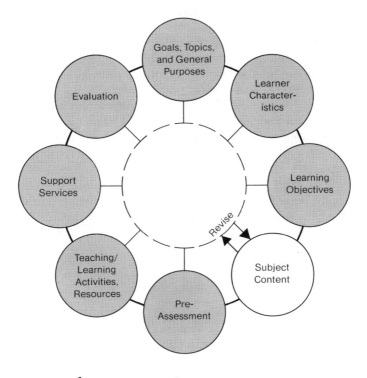

4 *Subject Content*

*What subject content should be treated
. . . or what subject content supports
each objective?*

A student's learning experiences must involve subject content. The content, in turn, must closely relate to the objectives and to the student's needs.

A definite structure is inherent in the subject content of some topics. Therefore, in those cases enumerating subject content helps in the formulation of the learning objectives. At other times, objectives can satisfactorily be stated first, as they are clearly evident from the topic's general purposes, and then details of content can be derived from the objectives. Employ whichever procedure you wish or whichever seems appropriate to your situation, always recognizing the close association of objectives and subject content.

In one sense, we might say that objectives are what you want content to do.

For many teachers, subject content is the traditional starting point for teaching. This is usual in subject-centered teaching. The textbook, as the primary instructional resource, often determines objectives, content, and teaching sequence.

In the plan we are developing, the textbook should be considered as only one source of subject content. Content in most subject areas is dynamic and changing, and is being reorganized as traditional courses are combined or as new courses are created around contemporary "theme topics," such as "Technology and Social Values," "Land Use and Ecology," or "Consumers' Purchasing Decisions." Therefore, teachers should also consider journal articles, pamphlets, documentary films, experienced consultants, and even their own practical experiences as other sources of subject content.

Organizing Content

What do I mean by the term *subject content* in the context of this instructional design plan? It comprises the selection and organizing of the specific knowledge (facts and information), skills (step-by-step procedures, conditions, and requirements), and attitudinal factors of any topic. If you make notes or prepare an outline of information for a lesson, a speech, or a report, you list subject content.

In considering levels of objectives, we examined the categories of learning behavior identified by Gagné. The four higher levels (facts, concepts, principles, and problem-solving) are essentially based on a sequential organization of subject content.

The lowest of them, *factual information* (the labeling, and simple description of objects or events), provides the foundation for knowledge of subjects or topics. When a number of facts can be identified as having a common property, learners reach the *concept* level. A child, for example, learns that three animals have common features, which lead the child to call all three, dogs—a concept. In studying maps, one can identify a number of landforms as peninsulas. Or one can examine the political structures of countries and arrive at the concept of democracy. Thus, concepts are the results of organizing information into meaningful structures.

A relationship between two or more concepts becomes a generalization, or principle. The formula $E = mc^2$ is the statement of a principle that combines the concepts E (energy), *m* (mass), and *c* (constant). Other principles are "warm air rises" (based on the concept of molecules and movement) and "tasteful artistic design" (using the concepts of simplicity, unity, emphasis, and balance). When students have learned a principle, they should be able to do more than simply restate the principle. They should be able to use it to deal with *problem situations*. These may require students to (1) explain events, (2) infer causes, (3) predict consequences, (4) control situations, (5) solve problems, and so on. The potential for such activities in the higher levels of the cognitive domain need to be considered as you select, organize, and sequence subject content.

You might find it useful to ask yourself questions like the following, as you prepare to list the content for a topic:

- What specifically must be taught or learned in this topic?
- What facts, concepts, and principles relate to this topic?
- What steps are involved in necessary procedures relating to this topic?
- What techniques are required in performing essential skills?

Answering questions like these is exactly how to select subject content. Under the appropriate headings enumerate all items of content you may find it necessary to use. (Do not hesitate to include more material than you may eventually need. It is easier to eliminate some items later than it is to find additional material on short notice after a program is underway.) Then check to see that the content and objectives are carefully interrelated, and proceed to your next planning step.

Anyone who has ever taught anything to someone else knows that, for learning to be successful, certain parts of any content must be mastered first, as a basis for subsequent learning. Subject matter may be organized and sequenced in various ways, depending on your topic and the manner in which you wish to handle the content. Some possibilities are suggested below:

- From known facts to new facts
- From the beginning of a process to its conclusion
- From a chronological point to a later point
- From a level of simple rote learning or an easy procedure to complex understandings or a more advanced manipulation
- From concrete, specific units of content to abstract levels of understanding, problem-solving, and reasoning

- From specific, separate facts, details, or observations to related concepts, principles, or other advanced generalizations (the inductive method of learning)
- Conversely, from stated principles and generalizations to facts, observations, and applications (the deductive method of learning)

The content in many topics does not necessarily follow a single linear sequence or a set order. Therefore, it may be necessary to choose items and determine order according to the emphasis you want in terms of the topic's general purposes. A specification table may help you organize your content in relation to the learning objectives (see page 35).

Task Analysis

In teaching skills, in vocational training, or in other procedural tasks, an organizational procedure called *task analysis* is often used. The term refers to a logical, step-by-step description of a job or performance skill such as learning to drive a car, baking bread, operating a piece of equipment, or performing a laboratory experiment. To make a task analysis, either a person experienced in performing the skill lists each element in the operation in sequence, or someone else observes the expert performing the activity and makes the list as he or she watches. By doing a thorough task analysis, you make sure all elements of a procedure are considered in the planning and will therefore be treated properly during instruction.

A task analysis for operating a drill press to bore holes in wood, for example, would be as follows:

1. Select bit for use.
2. Set motor speed according to the size of the bit.
3. Place bit in chuck.
4. Tighten bit with chuck key.
5. Remove key from chuck.
6. Place scrap of wood between table and stock to be bored.
7. Adjust the height of the table so bit is approximately one inch above stock to be bored.
8. Lock table.
9. Clamp stock to table, or hold stock flat and firmly.
10. Turn power on . . . and so forth.

The process of analyzing a task is an important way of identifying and then specifying subject content. It can help you state the subordinate objectives for a terminal objective. Such a listing may also be of particular use in preparing the script for audiovisual materials (a film, slides, videorecording).

When content is being selected, consideration might also be given to grouping the essential knowledge and skills that students should achieve on a *mastery* level, separately from those elements of subject matter that may be optional or required for achievement above the base mastery level (see page 93).

If you are planning a program to treat recent developments in a subject area or to integrate topics and content in new configurations (such as combining aspects of natural sciences and social sciences or language arts and drama), attempt to develop a new perspective for subject content—its selection, organization, and sequence.

Subject content for the sample topics is suggested below:

HAIKU

History of Haiku
1. Forms of Japanese poetry
   a. tanka, 31 syllables in five lines (5-7-5-7-7)
   b. *choka*, poems longer than five lines
   c. *sedoka*, special development of six lines
   d. *renga*, three or more poems making up link-verse sequences
   e. *haiku*, first three lines of tanka or renga
2. Historical Poets
   a. Matsuo Basho (1644–1694), greatest of the haiku poets, wrote his reactions to nature.
   b. Yosa Buson (1716–1784) wrote of the warmth of human affairs.
   c. Kobayashi Issa (1763–1828) emphasized the lives of the common people.
   d. Setchuan Jakushi (1848–1908) brought a modern approach to haiku composition.

Form of Haiku
1. First line, 5 syllables
2. Second line, 7 syllables
3. Third line, 5 syllables

Elements Common to Most Haiku
1. Refers to seasons of the year
2. Implies a relationship of human beings and nature
3. Expects the reader to feel the scene described, as something personal

SHEET-METAL CRAFT

Kinds of Sheet-Metal Work
1. Planning, layout, fabrication, assembly, and installation of metal products
   a. Surfaces
   b. Interior furnishings
   c. Exteriors of buildings
   d. Ducts
2. Determining sizes and types of metal or other materials
3. Using a variety of tools to cut and form metal
4. Performing cutting, forming, and other operations

Employment Opportunities
1. Fabrication plants
2. Custom-work shops
3. Installation contractors
4. Government agencies
5. Heavy industry
6. Self-employment

Monetary Advantages
1. Good hourly wage scale
2. Paid vacations, health and welfare funds, and pensions

Possible Future Advancement
1. Growing field of employment
2. Advancement to detailer or estimator
3. Further advancement possible to foreman, superintendent, or contractor
4. Self-employment

Recommended Educational Background
1. High school diploma (required)
2. Several semesters of math, including fractions and decimals, geometry, and trigonometry
3. Industrial arts

Apprenticeship (4 to 5 years)
1. Some individuals can acquire the skills of the trade through correspondence and trade-school courses or by learning from an experienced craftsman, but the usual way is to enter a formal apprenticeship program.

THE FUTURE

1. Major writings on the future
   Daniel Bell, *Toward the World 2000*
   Arthur Clarke, *Profiles of the Future*
   Don Fabun, *Dynamics of Change*
   Robert Heilbroner, *The Future as History*
   Herman Kahn, *Thinking About the Unthinkable*
   Herman Kahn and Anthony Weiner, *The Year 2000*
   John McHale, *The Future of the Future*
   Dennis Meadows, *The Limits of Growth*
   Gordon Taylor, *The Biological Time Bomb*
   Alvin Toffler, *Future Shock*
2. Possible areas of future change or development
   Behavior modification
   Land use
   Medical priorities
   Weather control
   Priorities in society
   Cities
   Politics tomorrow
   War and violence
   Use of outer space

Transportation
Communications
Shelter

OVERHEAD PROJECTION

Operating the Overhead Projector
1. Place machine at front of classroom, and stand beside it facing the class.
2. Controls: (a) on/off fan switch, (b) focus knob, (c) image-elevation knob

Types of Transparencies
1. Showing all content
2. Disclosing information by unmasking
3. Adding overlays to base sheet

Evaluating Commercial Transparencies
1. Accuracy of content
2. Makes good use of overhead features
3. Technical quality: (a) artwork, (b) lettering size and style, (c) use of color

Sources of Transparencies
1. Library file
2. Department collection
3. Commercial catalogs
4. National Information Center for Educational Media (NICEM) reference

Preparing Transparencies
1. Felt pens on acetate
2. Thermal film process: (a) carbon-based original, (b) infrared machine, (c) pass film and original through machine
3. Diazo film process: (a) opaque drawing on translucent paper, (b) expose drawing and film in ultraviolet light printer, (c) develop film in container of ammonia fumes

TECHNIQUE FOR WASHING HANDS

Routes by Which Bacteria Are Transmitted
1. Hospital equipment to patient or worker
2. Patient to patient
3. Worker to worker
4. Worker to patient
5. Patient to worker

Circumstances That Necessitate Washing Hands
1. Before and after contact with a patient
2. After contact with waste or contaminated materials
3. Before handling food or food receptacles
4. Any other time hands become soiled

Technique

1. Turn water on; adjust to warm temperature.
2. Wet hands.
3. Apply soap thoroughly, including under nails and between fingers.
4. Wash palms and backs of hands with ten strong movements.
5. Wash fingers and spaces between them with ten strokes.
6. Wash wrists, and up to three or four inches above the wrists with ten rotary actions.
7. Repeat Steps 3–6 for the remainder of two minutes.
8. Rinse well, with the final rinse moving from wrist to fingers.
9. Dry thoroughly with a paper towel from wrist to fingers.
10. Turn off water, using a paper towel to cover the faucet, and discard towel.

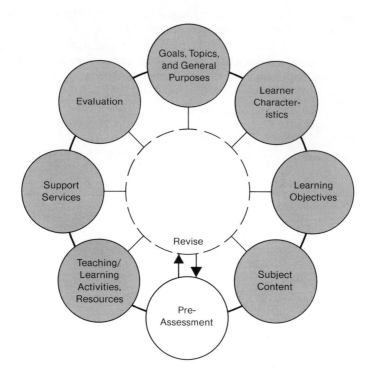

5 *Pre-Assessment*

*Does each student have the background preparation
to study this topic, and may he or she already
be proficient in what is to be taught?*

Now that you have examined learning objectives and the subject
content relating to them, it is time to ask two questions: (1) Is the
student prepared to study the topic or unit? and (2) Is the student
already competent in some of the stated objectives?

In traditional instruction, if people pay attention to such questions at all, they answer them by using placement and diagnostic
tests as ways of determining students' background in the subject
and as guides for grouping them.

Through data gathered about learner characteristics, you have already acquired general knowledge about the backgrounds of individual students. But in order to plan learning activities for which students are prepared and at the same time to ensure that learners do not waste their time on things they already know, it is important to find out specifically (1) to what extent each student has acquired the necessary prerequisites for studying the topic and (2) what the student may have already mastered about the subject to be studied. Pre-assessment can give you this information.

Prerequisite Testing

A *prerequisite test* determines whether students have the appropriate background preparation for the topic—for example, can the students perform basic arithmetic at a level that qualifies them to start learning algebra? It is useful to prepare a complete list of required competencies in order to establish the basis for constructing the prerequisite test. This test can be the paper-and-pencil kind (sometimes standardized tests are administered) or some other, more appropriate measuring method, like testing performance, reviewing a student's previous or related work, observing the student at work, or interviewing the student. (Further details on many testing methods are considered in Chapter 8, "Evaluation.")

The results of this prerequisite testing will indicate which students are fully ready for the topic, which ones need some remedial work, and which are not ready and should therefore start at a lower level.

Do not assume that grades in previous or related courses are necessarily accurate indicators of students' satisfactory preparation for your program. The objectives of courses at other schools may be quite different from what the titles or descriptions of those courses indicate. Do your own prerequisite evaluation.

Pretesting

A second reason for pre-assessing is to determine which of the objectives students may already have achieved. This is a *pretest* of the topic that is planned. It may be proper to select or adapt for the pretest, questions and problems from the evaluation instruments you are developing in the plan. Some authorities recommend using the actual evaluation tests (or modified forms of them) for both pretesting and final evaluation (called a *post-test*). In that case, the amount of student learning is determined from the gain in scores between pre- and post-tests. In the same sense, the post-test for one topic could serve as a prerequisite test for the next, related topic to be studied.

Instead of a formal test, you might use a pretopic questionnaire, or even an informal, oral questioning of the class ("How many of you have ever used a protractor?") and having the students reply with a show of hands, to determine students' experience with a topic. For mature students a questionnaire, in which each student indicates his or her level of skill or knowledge for all items to be studied, will go further than the few questions of a pretest.

For the more traditional group-instruction situation, in which students move together through all teacher-sequenced experiences, pre-assessing may be of little value. But if you plan to individualize instruction, then both the prerequisite test and the pretest are of particular importance for determining students' readiness and for indicating to both student and teacher the level at which a student should start a program. The pretest results enable the teacher to organize and schedule students with maximum efficiency. Pre-assessment also weeds out students who are not ready for the course and those who are already familiar with the material.

Other, secondary purposes may also be served by a pretest. For one thing, when students read pretest questions or otherwise experience what they will be learning, their interest may be aroused. This is certainly a legitimate reason for including a pretest in the instructional design plan. A related benefit is that a pretest gives students a good indication of what will be treated during the unit. Being aware, they are better prepared to move ahead.

When you pretest, however, be sure students understand the purpose. Taking any test is a traumatic experience for many students, and when they must reply to questions, problems, or situations with which they have little, if any, knowledge or experience, they may experience considerable frustration. Tell them clearly that the tests in no way count toward grades.

Finally, the results of pre-assessments may also affect instructional planning. It may be necessary to eliminate, modify, or add objectives to the program after the results are analyzed.

Examples of both prerequisite and pretest items for the sample topics appear below:

HAIKU

Prerequisite Quiz

1. From your past experience with poetry, tell whether the following sentences are true or false.
   a. In proper poetic form, the final two lines of a poem should rhyme.
   b. All lines in a poem contain the same number of syllables.
   c. Poetry is a method of expression found in the cultures of most countries.
   d. There are many different forms of poetry.

Pretest Questions

2. What country did the haiku verse form originate in?
   a. India
   b. China
   c. Japan
   d. Vietnam
3. Write the correct syllable form for haiku.
4. Which of the following are characteristic of most haiku?
   a. Treats a subject humorously
   b. Deals with the relationship between man and nature
   c. Deals with war and human suffering
   d. Identifies a season of the year
5. Have you ever written your own haiku?
   Note: For students who answer Questions 2, 3, and 4 correctly, Teacher Activity 2 may be optional.

SHEET-METAL CRAFT

Because the purpose of this topic is motivational and informational, the pre-assessment should measure what the student already knows about it and serve to interest him or her in it.

1. In which two of the following projects would a sheet-metal craftsperson work?
   a. Riveting the steel frame of a high-rise structure
   b. Making a church spire out of aluminum
   c. Building a plastic hull for a boat
   d. Constructing the ducts for an air-conditioning unit
2. Which of these tools are used in sheet-metal work?

strippers
pipe wrench
sander
pipe threader
snips
oscilloscope
air brush
jointer
hammer and anvil
power shears

3. Which statement(s) are true of the sheet-metal craft?
   a. A high school diploma is required.
   b. Apprenticeship is 6 to 8 years.
   c. You can become a journeyman after a successful apprenticeship.
   d. Welding and soldering are two metal-sealing operations.
   e. The joint apprenticeship committee in a community provides on-the-job experiences for individuals.

THE FUTURE

No formal testing or questioning is planned.

OVERHEAD PROJECTION

1. Have you used the overhead projector for instructional purposes? (If your answer is yes, reply to Questions 2 and 3.)
2. Describe briefly how extensive your experience has been.
3. How would you rate your ability to use the projector? (If you have had extensive, satisfactory experience with the projector, see your discussion group instructor for permission to skip laboratory practice with the projector.)
4. Have you made your own transparencies for teaching? (If you answer yes, reply to Questions 5 and 6.)
5. What techniques have you used?
6. Are any of these transparencies available? (If you feel you are experienced in preparing your own transparencies, discuss with your group instructor the possibility of skipping this part of the topic. You will still be expected to satisfy Objective 3 with transparencies you have already made or with new ones.)

TECHNIQUE FOR WASHING HANDS

1. Under which of the following circumstances is it necessary for you to wash your hands?
   a. After contact with a patient
   b. Before handling food
   c. After using a hand lotion
   d. After entering an operating room in surgical dress

2. Name three routes by which bacteria may be transmitted in a hospital.

3. List the steps you feel a hospital employee should take in washing his or her hands correctly.

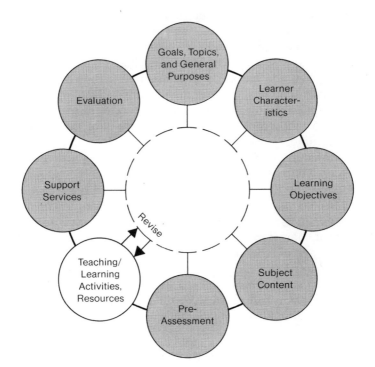

6 *Teaching/Learning Activities and Resources*

*What instructional methods and instructional
resources will be most appropriate for
accomplishing each objective?*

All the planning you have done up to this point has been preliminary to selecting the teaching/learning activities for your
instructional plan. You must determine the most efficient and effective methods and then select materials to provide learning experiences that will utilize the content associated with each objective. The terms *most efficient* and *most effective*, along with *the best
way*, are often used in education to describe what should be done.
These words have a fine intention, but they are actually value

statements without practical referents. Those who use them rarely go beyond stating them. Find "the best way" is usually left to the person implementing a program.

It is my purpose here to offer some bases on which to make decisions when you are ready to select the teaching activities, student learning activities, and instructional materials that will enable the largest possible number of students in your group to master the objectives at an acceptable level of achievement in a reasonable amount of time.

Unfortunately, there is no formula for matching activities to objectives. What may work for one teacher or with one group of students can be unsatisfactory in another situation. You need to know the strengths and weaknesses of alternative methods and of various materials. Then you can make your selections in terms of the student characteristics and needs that will *best* serve the objectives you have established.

After pilot tryouts and full-scale use, you will be able to answer such questions as, "Does the plan work?" and, "How well does it work?" Then you can make up your own mind about which instructional methods and materials are *most effective* and *efficient*.

Personnel Responsibilities

With some guidance, most teachers and teaching teams can determine their purposes, list learner characteristics, establish learning objectives, indicate content, prepare pre-assessments, and develop their evaluation methods.

In addition, teachers generally have the skill and experience to decide on instructional methods (particularly the methods applied in traditional classroom instruction, such as lectures, audiovisual presentations, class discussions, supervised group work, and independent study). But teachers may not be familiar with newer forms of presentation and independent learning activities. Qualified professional help may be required for making decisions about when and how to implement newer methods. At this point the role of the instructional designer becomes particularly important.

The selection of instructional materials is closely associated with the planning of teaching and learning activities, both of which should be considered together. Because of the wide variety of audiovisual and related materials now available, no one teacher or even an experienced teaching team can know the strengths and best uses of them all. Many technological resources (such as audio cassette recordings, compressed speech recordings, videotape recordings, Super 8 mm film, still/motion film combinations, microprint forms, synchronized slide/tape and filmstrip/tape materials, multi-image devices, and multimedia instructional kits) require in-depth knowledge for selection, planning, preparation, and use. The great majority of teachers do not have this knowledge, and they have little time to acquire it.

The instructional designer, in addition to the other responsibilities in instructional planning, should be able to provide the professional guidance necessary for selecting instructional resources. The designer may be assisted by a qualified media (audiovisual) specialist who is knowledgeable about the characteristics of nonprint resources. (Additional roles and responsibilities of instructional planners are considered in Chapter Y.)

Teaching/Learning Patterns

There are many roads to learning. No doubt, you are familiar with the general patterns of teaching and learning. Traditionally, teachers *present* information to groups of students through lecturing, talking informally, writing on the chalkboard, demonstrating, and showing audiovisual materials. Students work *individually* by reading the text, solving problems, writing reports, using the library, working in labs or shops, and possibly by viewing films and other visuals or listening to recordings. *Interaction* between teacher and students and among students takes place by means of discussions (usually in the form of questions and answers) and small-group activities, student projects, and reports.

These three patterns—presentation to a group, individualized learning, and teacher-student interaction—are the basic methods of teaching and learning. Each instructional activity, whether teacher-controlled or for independent student use, is related to one of these patterns.

Today teachers no longer look upon these three patterns casually when structuring an instructional program. Why is this so?

First, there is the question of efficiency in the use of student time, facilities, and equipment. It may be more efficient for certain purposes to present information to a group of students (of any size) at one time than to have each student study the material independently. This not only saves time, but can lessen the wear and tear on equipment and materials caused by repeated use. It also permits teachers more time for small groups, for individual tutoring and consultation, and for instructional planning.

Second, we know that many students can learn quite satisfactorily on their own, at their own pace, whereas other students prefer highly structured teaching/learning situations in which they are systematically guided through a lesson. These variations among students require that various methods of instruction be employed.

Third, when we consider the newer methods of instruction, we must take into account the fact that the impersonal features of the group presentation and individualized learning techniques often keep students from direct contact with the teacher. Therefore, in order to assure some opportunity for face-to-face teacher-student relationships, it is important to make use of small-group interaction in learning.

From an overall consideration, the group presentation and individualized learning patterns may work satisfactorily to achieve objectives in the cognitive and psychomotor categories. Although some attention can be given to objectives relating to attitudes and appreciations in presentations and independent study activities, the best way to deal with affective objectives is through cooperative group activities. Through the give-and-take of discussions, students can be motivated and helped to sharpen their judgments and discriminations, to deal with novel situations and unexpected happenings, and to approach attitudinal objectives, which we find so hard to state in precisely measurable terms.

For these and other reasons, an understanding of the three teaching/learning patterns is necessary to instructional planning. Shortly, I will examine them in detail. But, first, attention needs to be given to some general principles of learning.

Principles of Learning

In recent years research into the elements of human learning has developed generalizations that can be applied in planning instructional programs. Many of these principles are derived from the work of behavioral psychologists, who interpret human behavior largely as connections between stimuli and responses. This concept is implicit in the "programmed instruction" approach introduced by B. F. Skinner and his colleagues. Most learning psychologists agree with the following principles:

1. PRELEARNING PREPARATION Students should have satisfactorily achieved the learning that is prerequisite to the lesson. Unless the former learning has been soundly acquired, the subsequent learning may be rote and not easily related by the individual to the unit or the total course structure.

2. MOTIVATION When a student perceives some personal value in a topic or learning task, or if a desire to learn about the topic can be encouraged, the student's attention will be captured and held. The result is that teaching and learning are easier and the student can be led to accept responsibility for pursuing learning experiences independently. Students' interest can be maintained by providing a variety of learning experiences.

3. INDIVIDUAL DIFFERENCES Students learn at various rates and within a class or group the variations can be considerable. Therefore, learning experiences should be designed so that students may proceed at their own paces and possibly on their own levels of ability, using materials that are most appropriate for them.

4. INSTRUCTIONAL CONDITIONS Successful learning is more likely when objectives are clearly stated for students and when learning activities are carefully sequenced in relation to those objectives. Students can acquire more information and retain it longer when they have objectives that are meaningful and systematically organized. This also means that content should be organized sequentially from simple to complex—that is, starting with factual learning, then moving on to concept formation, principles, and eventually to higher intellectual levels, such as problem-solving, prediction, and inference. Both inductive ("inquiry" and "discovery") and deductive methods of treating subject matter should be employed.

5. ACTIVE PARTICIPATION Learning must be *performed* by the student and not by the teacher through some kind of transmission. Therefore, for successful learning, a student should be directed systematically to participation activities. The teacher's main function is to organize and make the materials available to students in the best possible form.

6. SUCCESSFUL ACHIEVEMENT Learning must be structured in such a way that the student is mentally challenged and frequently successful. As students find out they are successful,

they experience satisfaction that motivates them to continue their efforts.

7. KNOWLEDGE OF RESULTS   Motivation for learning can be increased when students are informed of how well they are doing during the course of a lesson (often through self-check exercises, tests, informal discussions, and so forth). Thus, there must be many opportunities for students to test themselves. This provides feedback. When the results are positive, students are reinforced for continued effort.

8. PRACTICE   Closely associated with success and the knowledge of results is the need to provide opportunities for students to use their newly acquired knowledge and skills in many situations. Thus, once principles and generalizations are attained, then exercises and practical applications should be available.

9. RATE OF PRESENTING MATERIAL   The rate and amount of material to be learned at any one time or in any one lesson, must be related to the complexity and difficulty of the material in terms of the abilities of the students. Here especially, individual differences should be considered. The presentation of short segments of subject content, with many opportunities for student participation, practice, and self-testing, is an effective procedure for "programming" instructional sequences.

10. INSTRUCTOR'S ATTITUDE   A positive attitude on the parts of the teacher and any assistant can influence the attitudes of students toward the acceptance of new instructional procedures.

Some of these principles apply to each of the three teaching/learning patterns, but many of them are particularly necessary in the development of individualized learning activities. I will refer to these principles as I examine each teaching/learning pattern.

Group Presentation

In using the group-presentation pattern, the teacher or a student tells, shows, demonstrates, dramatizes, or otherwise presents subject content to a student group of any size. This can be done in the classroom, the lecture hall, or the auditorium. The teacher, in front of the group, may simply talk. He or she may also utilize audiovisual materials, such as transparencies, recordings, slides, or motion pictures, singly or in combination, as in multi-image presentations for motivational or inspirational purposes. (Some rather elaborate facilities have been constructed that allow a speaker to operate projection equipment by remote control, which makes it possible to show the materials at the teacher's own pace or automatically on cue.) The presentation can also take place without the teacher's being physically present, if the presentation is on film, audiotape with slides, or videotape.

Each of these methods illustrates the one-way transmission of a presentation—from teacher to students for a constant period of time (generally, one class period). In smaller classes there may be some degree of two-way communication between teacher and students. Students are generally passive receivers of information. They may be mentally active, but their outward physical movements are limited.

Since learning takes place best when students are active, it is desirable to incorporate student participation activities in the presentation format. By participation I mean that students either make physical movements or are challenged mentally to do something.

In a lecture or other such presentation, student participation can fall into three categories:

1. ACTIVE INTERACTION WITH THE INSTRUCTOR Asking and answering questions; entering into discussion with the instructor and other students; and consulting with the instructor after the presentation
2. WORKING AT THE STUDENT'S SEAT Taking notes, completing worksheets on topics as the presentation proceeds (filling in an outline of content, completing diagrams that accompany visual materials, writing replies to questions, solving problems, and making applications of content), and completing self-check exercises or quizzes
3. OTHER MENTAL PARTICIPATION Thinking along with the instructor, mentally verbalizing answers to rhetorical or direct questions and problems posed by the instructor and other students, and formulating questions to ask

Some instructors use simple mechanical-response devices that feed back to the instructors tabulations of student replies to objective questions during the session. Rather complex electronic equipment is used at some institutions for this purpose. This procedure not only keeps the student mentally active and indicates the amount of learning taking place, but it also lets the instructor know of any weak spots in the presentation.

When a teacher lectures, demonstrates, shows a film, or otherwise presents subject content to a class of students, the assumption is made that all students are acquiring the same understanding, to the same level of comprehension, at the same time. They are being forced to learn in lockstep at a pace set by the teacher. We know this is not the way learning actually takes place. Each student learns at an individual pace, to his or her own degree of understanding. The group presentation therefore often is not the way to provide satisfactory learning experiences when the purpose of instruction is the acquisition of information.

The current trend is to reduce the amount of time spent in teachers' presentations, in favor of devoting more time to individual study and to group activities. Thus, students are actively engaged in learning most of the time. Nevertheless, presentations can still accomplish the following:

- Introduce topics, discuss objectives, and provide orientation to other activities
- Create interest among students in a subject or topic
- Illustrate how a topic can be integrated with other topics and other subject areas
- Point out special applications of a subject and introduce developments in the field
- Present information not easily accessible to students
- Provide special enrichment materials and such resources as guest speakers and films that would not be available to small groups or individual students
- Provide opportunities for special student presentations

Individualized Learning

Of the three teaching and learning patterns, individualized learning has received the most attention from persons interested in revising instructional procedures recently. As the principles of learning indicate, there is much evidence to support the theory that learning must be accomplished by individuals for themselves and that it takes place best when students work at their own rates, are actively involved in performing specified tasks, and experience success. This means that, ideally, a separate set of learning experiences for each objective should be designed for each student, according to that student's individual characteristics and needs. Some experiments involving computer-based instruction are moving in this direction. By recognizing that active participation is a key element for learning, most teachers can design experiences for students that range from casual methods, through a carefully structured program, to one that allows students virtually complete freedom and responsibility for choosing, or even developing, their own experiences and materials according to their own learning styles.

Individualized learning patterns (some of them specialized) are also called by such labels as *self-instruction, independent study, individualized prescribed instruction,* and *self-directed* or *self-paced learning.* The important features for the student are self-responsibility, self-pacing, and successful learning, all based on specified learning objectives agreed to or selected by the student, and a variety of activities with accompanying resources. There is evidence that students participating in individualized learning programs are more interested and enthusiastic toward the subject, more independent and less restricted in their thinking, and more resourceful in their overall approach to learning than students in conventional school programs.

The kinds of learning objectives that may be suitably served by individualized learning include the following:

- Learning factual information
- Mastering concepts and principles
- Applying information, concepts, and principles
- Developing basic problem-solving skills
- Developing psychomotor skills

Thus, most of the levels in both the cognitive and psychomotor domains, as well as those in the Gagné hierarchy, can be treated through some types of individualized learning activities. Some of these categories of objectives should also be reinforced and supplemented by group-interaction activities. Topics or objectives that are highly abstract and not quantifiable, like philosophical thought, may be more appropriate for study in group-interaction sessions. But even with those, there is usually some fundamental, factual information that should be mastered before ideas are shared. And such basic material can be mastered through individualized study.

Within the framework of individualized learning certain procedures are applied. As students work by themselves, they do so without the intervention of the teacher, unless they request it. When students know little about a subject, it is essential that their learning experiences be carefully constructed and detailed. Programmed instruction has taught that individualized learning best takes place when content is structured in comparatively small, discrete steps, each one treating a single concept. The size of the steps can vary somewhat. It is essential, however, that they be carefully sequenced and that the material treated be precisely organized. Then the student's mastery of each step must be checked before the student proceeds to the next one. To do this, it is necessary to question or otherwise challenge the student to demonstrate the new understanding. The learner then receives immediate confirmation (feedback) of the correctness of the reply or other effort. With success, the learner confidently proceeds. When difficulties arise, further study may be necessary, or the student may ask the teacher for help. Thus, in individualized learning the student is continually challenged, experiences success, and learns the results of the efforts immediately.

In planning for individualized learning, many approaches are possible. The simplest is to design a single track for all students and select whatever instructional materials are required from among existing commercial ones (printed materials, filmstrips, recordings, 8 mm films, and so forth). Most of these materials are presentation devices, however. To provide for student participation, the teacher can develop worksheets or other aids that require students to respond to or act on the material. The main variable in this approach is *time.* Self-paced instruction allows most students—low achievers and slow learners, average learners, and high-level achievers—to attain many of the same competencies. This takes varying amounts of time, but with success even low achievers can build confidence in their accomplishments.

A more advanced way to develop individualized learning is to start with a variety of materials serving the objectives and then structure more than one instructional sequence with them in order to provide for the individual differences of students. Some students may take the fast track, even skipping ahead and using few materials before reaching the final evaluation step. Other students may require slower tracks that contain a greater number of concrete illustrations or examples, more review exercises, or even smaller segments of subject matter with a repetition of explanations in different contexts.

A set of three differently paced paths may be advisable. This plan enables the learner (in consultation with the teacher) to select a path to follow, but it leaves viable alternatives if the goals are too high or too low.

As we know, individuals differ in their learning styles. Some students respond best to visual materials. Others work better with verbal or mechanical techniques. Eventually, research should find the best way to match individual characteristics and learning styles, to enable each student to pursue his or her objective in the most efficient way possible.

In a high-level program it may be advisable to prepare an extensive package of materials and allow selected, mature students complete freedom to use them in the ways best suited to their individual styles or even to design their own learning experiences. For example, if the objective is to operate a piece of laboratory equipment, the program for mastering this objective may include an 8 mm film, a set of still pictures with captions, a programmed booklet, and actual practice with the equipment. One student might choose to begin with the film and then go immediately to the actual practice; another might prefer to read the booklet first and then look at the still pictures before attempting to practice; a third might practice at the outset or just read the booklet.

Many approaches to individualized learning are being explored and utilized on various educational levels around the country. Programs may include the use of simple, locally prepared materials or adaptations of commercial materials, or they may be full-scale and systematically planned local or commercial programs. A range of methods and resources is suggested below:

- STUDENT CONTRACTS The learner enters into an agreement with the teacher to achieve acceptable objectives, often by completing a project in exchange for rewards (credit points, participation in special activities, or free time). The teacher either suggests resources, or the student takes responsibility for deciding how to satisfy objectives and carry out the project.
- TEXTBOOK/WORKSHEETS Objectives are developed from textbook content with a worksheet directing the study of text chapters and providing review questions. Self-check applications occur often.

- AUDIOTAPE/WORKBOOK   A tape directs study in terms of objectives and refers the student to the printed workbook for information and exercises. The workbook may include verbal, diagrammatic, and pictorial materials. The tape may provide elaboration of content and feedback on answers. Self-check tests appear in the workbook. Both locally prepared and commercial tape/workbook programs are used.

- VISUAL MATERIALS/GUIDE SHEETS   This combination is useful for learning operational procedures, manipulative skills, and other visually demonstrable sequential activities. A series of photographs, Super 8 mm film, or a videotape can be prepared to demonstrate a procedure or skill, with detailed review on a guide sheet.

- PROGRAMMED INSTRUCTION BOOKLET   This generally consists of a statement of objectives and a series of printed frames that present small increments of subject content in a linear or branching sequence. The learner responds periodically to questions that test his or her understanding of the content. Knowledge of results is thus provided immediately. At the end of a sequence or program, the total learning is tested. Although some programmed instruction booklets are prepared locally, most of those in use are from commercial sources. (Note: This programmed approach to instruction is often incorporated in many of the other individualized learning methods described on these pages.)

- COMMERCIAL INSTRUCTIONAL PACKAGES   Materials such as slide series or filmstrips (silent or sound), recordings alone, or Super 8 mm films are developed in terms of topic objectives. Guide sheets provide directions for studying (by sections), review questions, and self-check tests.

- PROJECT PLAN (PROGRAM FOR LEARNING IN ACCORDANCE WITH NEEDS)   This is a commercially available school program in various subject areas. Program choices are based on objectives the student selects with the help of the teacher after reviewing the record of the student's accomplishments, which has been stored in a computer. Modules include approximately five objectives, with learning experiences based on commercial materials. Each module includes several alternative teaching/learning units, to provide for the differences in students' interests and learning styles. Tests measure achievement in each module.

- INDIVIDUALLY PRESCRIBED INSTRUCTION (IPI)   This is a comprehensive commercial elementary-grade program based on objectives and a detailed diagnosis of students' skills and abilities. Each child's work is guided by written prescriptions to meet that child's needs and interests. IPI includes daily monitoring of learners' progress by means of a computer. Commercial materials include study guides, most resources, worksheets, and tests.

- PERSONALIZED SYSTEM OF INSTRUCTION (PSI) OR KELLER PLAN   This is a program developed by psychologist Fred Keller and used mainly in college education. It is most frequently based on a textbook and study units prepared by the instructor. Each unit includes an introduction, objectives, reading assignments, study questions, and readiness tests. After studying independently, a student takes a readiness test administered by a student proctor. The proctor immediately grades the test and discusses the results with the student. If further study is necessary, the student takes another form of the text afterwards, repeating the procedure until successful. The learner then proceeds to the next unit.

- AUDIO-TUTORIAL SYSTEM (AT)   This approach was developed by S. N. Postlethwait, a botanist at Purdue University. It is used extensively in high school and college science courses, but the method can be applied in most cognitive-based subjects on all educational levels. The program involves using self-instructional learning carrels, and includes a study guide containing objectives, activities, exercises, and self-check tests. An audiotape leads the student through the learning experiences. The recorded tape is not a lecture, but consists of informal tutorial remarks and directions from instructor to student. Activities directed by the tape may include reading pages in books and articles, studying visual materials, handling objects, and working with demonstration materials. Both commercial and locally prepared units are utilized. The instructor or a teaching assistant is available in the learning center to assist students and answer questions. In addition to the self-instructional phase, there are small-group discussion and quiz sections, and infrequent general meetings.

- SELF-LEARNING MODULE (SLM), OR MINICOURSE   Many terms are used for self-contained instructional packages that treat single topics or units of subject matter and require from a few hours to a week of study time. A series of modules or minicourses can comprise a full-semester course, but flexibility may permit a student to select one or a few modules to serve specific instructional needs. Many modules are portable and can be used outside the classroom or laboratory. Complete modules generally include most elements of an instructional design plan as described in this book.

There are many publications on individualized learning that may give you further ideas for your own explorations. Some of the more noteworthy are listed under "Individualized Learning" in the Bibliography.

If you are developing an individualized learning program, the following checklist of questions to consider in evaluating your planning may prove helpful:

1. How many options do learners have in selecting their objectives and in choosing their own learning experiences and resources?
2. To what extent does the program adapt to characteristics of learners of differing cultural and ethnic backgrounds?
3. To what extent are learners identified who need remedial help before starting on the unit or module?
4. To what extent are learners allowed to skip ahead if they already show competence in part of the module?
5. To what extent are low-level cognitive and psychomotor skills used to provide higher-level learning experiences and practical applications of subject content?
6. To what degree are learners permitted or encouraged to progress at their own rates?
7. To what extent do learners have opportunities for checking their progress?
8. How much attention is given to attitude-formation?
9. To what extent do students have opportunities to share their learning or otherwise interact among themselves and with the teacher?
10. To what extent do teachers consult or assist individual learners and small groups?
11. To what extent will you test the effectiveness of the module before you give it full use with a class?

In summary, individualized learning offers a number of unique advantages as an instructional method. Its major contributions include the following:

- Responsibility for learning rests with the student, through active participation.
- The study habits and the independence may carry over to students' other educational activities and personal behaviors.
- Subject content can be treated in more innovative and effective ways than they can in conventional instruction.
- Most cognitive learning tasks and many psychomotor skills can be accomplished more efficiently than in conventional instruction.
- Each student participates at his or her own convenience and pace.
- It allows both slow learners and advanced students to pursue studies, each on his or her own level of ability and learning conditions.
- The number of failures or unsatisfactory performances can be appreciably reduced.
- Both variety and flexibility are more possible.
- A successful individualized learning program can allow for more attention to the individual student, personal contact with the instructor, and interaction with other students.

There are also some limitations to individualized learning, which should be recognized, as well:

- There may be a lack of interaction between instructor and students or among students if this is the sole method of instruction or if opportunities for contact with instructor are not provided.
- If a single-path, lockstep method is followed, learning can be monotonous and uninteresting.
- This is not a suitable method for all students or for all instructors.
- Students' procrastination or delays in completing work may have to be overcome.
- This often requires team planning and coordination with extensive support services, in contrast to being a one-person operation and thus may be complex and costly.

As teachers plan informal or fully designed individualized learning programs, they should recognize that not only will they be changing their methods of instruction, but they must change their own roles with students. These can become both more stimulating and more demanding. Some of the changes that can be anticipated are suggested below:

- freedom from routine teaching of basic facts and skills
- more time spent with individual students in diagnosing their difficulties, giving help, and monitoring their progress
- more opportunities to interact with students on higher intellectual levels concerning their problems, interests, and uses of the subject content
- more time required for preparing, gathering, and organizing materials for students
- more time required to orient and supervise aides, tutors, proctors, and other assistants

Interaction Between Teacher and Students

In the interaction teaching/learning pattern, teachers and students—or students themselves—work together in small groups to discuss, question, pursue problems cooperatively, and report. The importance of interaction cannot be overemphasized. It gives students and teachers an opportunity to get to know each other face-to-face. To be of maximum benefit to students, the interaction group should consist of no more than twelve persons—from eight to twelve participants seems to be ideal.

The interaction group should carry on discussions that review, clarify, correct, reinforce, and apply the learning that has resulted from individualized learning and group presentations. Students can report on their projects and other learning experiences, which enables them to learn from each other as well as from the teacher. Small-group sessions may also be used to test students' understandings of the concepts and principles they have acquired during the course of study.

Other areas of small-group activity may be entirely student-directed. These activities may encompass committee and team planning, research, construction, tryouts for presentations, and self-evaluations. Students may also study films and other materials and engage in their own interaction without a teacher present.

The interaction-group meeting is *not* a time for a lecture or any other lengthy presentation. Instructors who are unprepared or who are inexperienced with this type of activity may fall back on lecturing for their own security. Much practice is sometimes necessary before a teacher can successfully become a *participating* member of the group rather than the *dominating* member.

In interaction groups instructors may have available some of the audiovisual materials and other resources used in group presentations and individualized study. This can be useful when questions are raised and points amplified.

I have already noted some of the particular strengths of small groups in achieving objectives in the affective area—attitude formation, development of appreciations, cooperation, and interpersonal relations. In the cognitive domain higher-level skills like problem-solving and decision-making can receive attention through interaction sessions. Role-playing, simulations, gaming, and case studies are valuable vehicles for treating these higher skills, while at the same time aiding in attitude formation.

Other values derive from teacher/student interaction as well. These include experiences in listening and in oral expression when students organize and present their ideas. The more able students can strengthen their own learning by explaining points or principles to other students (peer tutoring). Students can also practice leadership. Students who need encouragement can be recognized, and those students who are making poor progress can be identified. Also, during small-group sessions instructors can become aware of the successes or shortcomings of various phases of the instructional program and can obtain suggestions from students for revisions.

The three patterns we have been examining—group presentation, individualized learning, and teacher/student interaction activities—provide the framework within which planning for learning takes place. The following important questions should be asked:

- Is there subject content that can best be uniformly presented to all students at one time?
- Is there subject content that students can better study on their own, at their individual paces?
- Are there experiences that would be served by discussion or other group activity, with or without a teacher present?

- Is there need for individual student-teacher discussion or consultation in private?

In considering these questions, the teacher should realize that a plan needs to have some degree of balance among the three teaching/learning patterns. Some enthusiasts recommend that individualized learning, for example, is proper activity 100 percent of the time. Others believe that suitable opportunities must be available for teacher-student contact and group interaction. The major trend is, however, to reduce the time spent in presentations to groups, to give students increased responsibilities for individualized learning, but also to provide for sufficient interaction experiences, as well.

In many situations there are no clearcut divisions among the three patterns. A presentation to a regular-size class can incorporate questions and discussion. An individualized learning session may be supplemented periodically with tutorial interaction as one student helps another or as the teacher replies to a student's question. But this is how it should be. Use each pattern at the right time for its best service to learning.

In using these teaching/learning patterns, it will be helpful to consider two questions in order to develop two categories of activities: (1) *What will the teacher do?* Some activities are conducted by the teacher as presentations to a group, such as an explanation with materials shown on an overhead projector; other activities are controlled by the teacher through small-group interaction, such as a review discussion. (2) *What will the student do?* Some activities are the responsibility of the students as they work by themselves, such as reading, laboratory work, and completing worksheets; other activities are the responsibility of the students when they are active members of a small group—for example, reporting, replying, being tested.

Obviously, under an individualized learning program most of the activity is performed by students. The teacher participates in small-group interaction sessions when reports, discussions, and evaluations take place. Therefore, in your planning at this stage, indicate the *two* categories *(teacher activities* and *student activities)* under the heading "Teaching/Learning Activities." As you consider each objective, ask yourself if this objective can be most readily achieved by a teacher activity, a student activity, or by a combination. Then, specify the details of the activity for the teacher, the students, or both.

For example, in a course on meteorology for a unit on weather air masses, the teacher presents to the class a series of transparencies that show the features of various air masses, their places of origin, and so forth. This activity would come under the heading *Teacher Activities*. Each student completes a worksheet during the presentation, and following it reviews the topic by studying a filmstrip independently. These are *Student Activities*. All of this is placed under the major heading of "Teaching/Learning Activities and Resources."

Instructional Resources

Closely associated with the selection of teacher and student activities is the selection of supporting materials that can motivate students and can effectively explain and illustrate subject content. These resources include printed materials of many kinds, audiovisual media, and other items for group and individual uses. For lists of commonly used resources see the charts on pages 77–79.

Members of planning teams have generally had experience with using such traditional materials as textbooks, reference books, magazines, pamphlets, workbooks, and microforms of these and other printed items. But, even though audiovisual and related resources are proving to be particularly useful for instruction, teachers' knowledge and judgment concerning the advantages, limitations, and special applications of these materials are limited.

In the past, the failure of many innovative instructional media to improve teaching and learning was frequently attributed to the shortcomings of the media themselves. This was particularly true of language laboratories, instructional television, and some forms of programmed instructional materials. But in actuality the failures were often caused by the inadequate design of programs, ones that failed to consider all interdependent factors of the instructional plan before selecting appropriate instructional media. In many instructional situations today—particularly in individualized learning—media are no longer supplementary to instruction, but instead provide the main instructional input. It can be more efficient in terms of learning for the student *to see* a place, a function, or a relationship than to just hear about it or read about it. Furthermore, today's students relate as much or more directly to picture images and sound than they do to the printed word.

For years educational researchers have been pondering such questions as: "Is there a medium or a combination of media that would be best for teaching a particular subject?" and, "Can media be classified according to their effectiveness for teaching certain kinds of facts, concepts, principles, or other generalizations?" No simple answers have been forthcoming. Much of the research into learning with audiovisual materials has been inconclusive, or even contradictory. What has resulted is evidence that certain learning experiences might be accomplished equally well by any of a number of media. On the other hand, it has also been shown that a medium that is well adapted for one instructional function may be unsatisfactory for a second, different function within the same instructional sequence. This suggests that a variety of materials may have to be selected for a given program, with each one doing specifically what it can best do at a specific point in the learning sequence.

Selecting Media

Our task of selecting media is complicated, for three reasons. First, there are many audiovisual resources from which to choose. Second, there are no clearcut guidelines for making a selection. Third, few educators have had broad enough experience with the resources available to have a sound basis for selecting an appropriate medium or combination of media for communicating content or providing student experiences, in terms of an objective within a chosen teaching/learning pattern.

Many teachers select media on the basis of what they are most comfortable or familiar with. However, when you consider the questions listed below, you may find that one medium is clearly preferable in certain situations.

1. WILL THE MATERIAL BE PRESENTED TO A GROUP, OR WILL IT BE USED FOR INDIVIDUALIZED LEARNING? Some audiovisual materials are best used for presentations. Others are more suitable for individualized learning, but most can be adapted to either use.

2. DOES THE CONTENT REQUIRE GRAPHIC TREATMENT (DESIGN, ARTWORK, OR LETTERING), PHOTOGRAPHY (STILL OR MOTION), OR A COMBINATION OF GRAPHICS AND PHOTOGRAPHY? Graphics (diagrams, cartoons, charts) can clarify and simplify

complex concepts, but for some needs the truer reality of a photographic form (photographs, slides, motion pictures) may be required. It usually requires more time to prepare graphic visuals than it does to make photographic materials.

3. SHOULD A VISUAL BE PRESENTED IN THE FORM OF STILL PICTURES OR AS A MOTION PICTURE? A motion picture is a "transient" medium, requiring students to grasp the message as the film is projected. A still picture is a "persistent" medium, permitting students to study the message at their own paces. It takes more skill, time, and money to prepare a motion picture than it does to make still materials.

4. WHAT KINDS OF STILL PICTURES ARE AVAILABLE? For instructional purposes, still pictures may be prepared in the form of photographic prints on paper, black-and-white or color slides, filmstrips, transparencies for overhead projection, or microforms (such as microfiche). Each form has advantages and limitations in preparation and use.

5. SHOULD A MOTION PICTURE BE PREPARED ON 16 MM OR SUPER-8 MM FILM OR ON VIDEOTAPE? There is no difference in learning from a 16 mm or 8 mm film or from videotape. One can be readily converted to the other form with adequate results, as long as the original is of high quality. When synchronous sound (for lip movement and voices) is necessary, videotape may be less complex and costly to produce than 16 mm film.

6. SHOULD THE VISUAL MATERIAL BE ACCOMPANIED BY RECORDED SOUND? When used with visuals, sound on tape or film can direct attention, explain details, raise questions, and make transitions from one picture or idea to the next. On the other hand, some subjects can be treated so they have suitable impact without using sound for explanation. If necessary, explanatory material can be put on paper to accompany silent materials. If synchronized sound and pictures are used (which means that an inaudible signal on tape controls picture changes), the opportunity for a student to go back and review the narration, picture, or both, at will is eliminated. By verbally indicating when picture changes should be made, the student is free to go back at any time and then easily move ahead with pictures and sound together.

7. WHEN SHOULD THE USE OF MULTIMEDIA TECHNIQUES BE CONSIDERED? Multimedia methods are used in presentations when more than one medium such as transparencies and

slides, presented together or sequentially, can best explain and illustrate content. Such presentations are complex to plan and prepare but can be highly effective for instruction. To serve different learning styles of individual students, a variety of media may also be assigned sequentially or be made available for selection.

8. WHAT DECISIONS MUST BE MADE WHEN SELECTING EQUIPMENT?   When deciding on materials, consider these matters relating to equipment for use with the materials. First, determine whether the equipment will be for teachers or students to use. Equipment to be used repeatedly by students may have to be simpler to operate and more durable than that for teachers to use in presentations. Second, determine what technical specifications and special features are required or desirable. Consider how the equipment is to be used with the materials in the assigned facility. Then examine the makes and models that will best serve the purposes. Finally, find out what the equipment will cost. If the price is higher than the budget will permit, you may have to lower your requirements, reduce the number of units by having students share equipment for certain work, or revise your instructional plan and the materials it requires, to eliminate the equipment or make substitutions.

The three media-selection diagrams that follow can guide you to answers to some of these questions.[1] Each diagram is a sequence chart for a teaching/learning pattern and in terms of the objectives a medium will serve, can lead you to a group of related media from which you can make a final choice.

[1] Jerrold E. Kemp, *Planning and Producing Audiovisual Materials* (New York: T. Y. Crowell, 1975), p. 49.

Diagrams for Media Selection

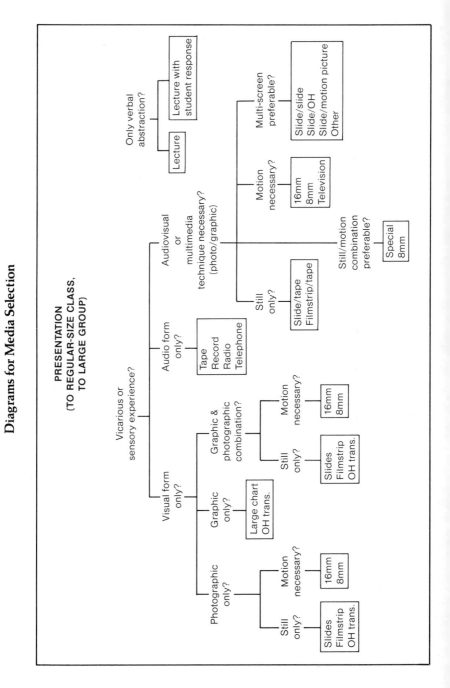

Diagrams for Media Selection (*continued*)

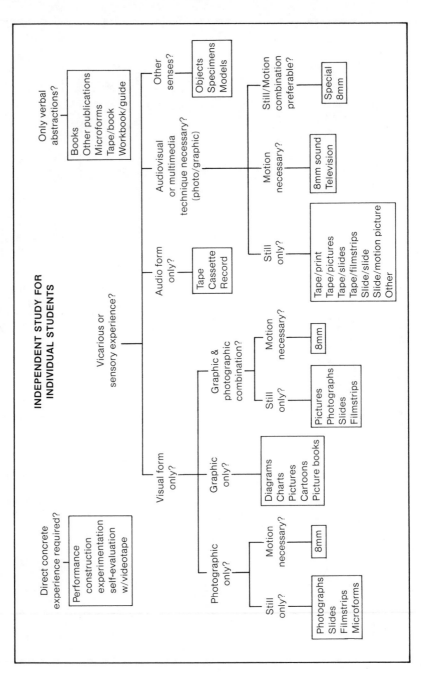

INDEPENDENT STUDY FOR INDIVIDUAL STUDENTS

Direct concrete experience required?

Performance
construction
experimentation
self-evaluation
w/videotape

Vicarious or sensory experience?

Visual form only?

Photographic only?

Still only?

Photographs
Slides
Filmstrips
Microforms

Motion necessary?

8mm

Graphic only?

Diagrams
Charts
Pictures
Cartoons
Picture books

Graphic & photographic combination?

Still only?

Pictures
Photographs
Slides
Filmstrips

Motion necessary?

8mm

Audio form only?

Tape
Cassette
Record

Audiovisual or multimedia technique necessary? (photo/graphic)

Still only?

Tape/print
Tape/pictures
Tape/slides
Tape/filmstrips
Slide/slide
Slide/motion picture
Other

Motion necessary?

8mm sound
Television

Still/Motion combination preferable?

Special
8mm

Only verbal abstractions?

Books
Other publications
Microforms
Tape/book
Workbook/guide

Other senses?

Objects
Specimens
Models

Diagrams for Media Selection (*continued*)

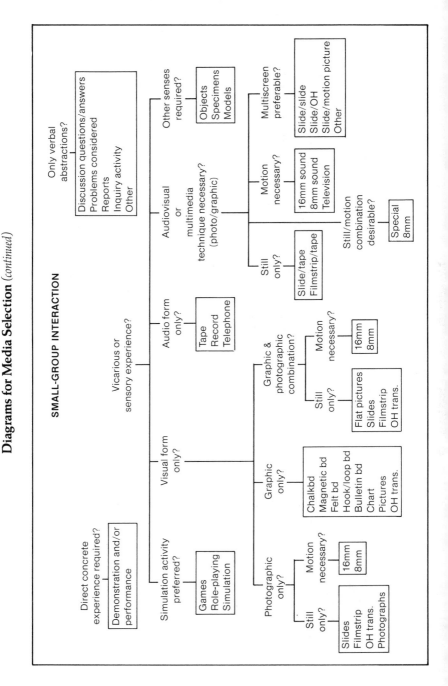

Making the Final Decision on Media

How can you determine which is the best audiovisual medium or combination of media to select in a particular situation?

In serving some objectives there is a clearcut *best* medium. If your need is to have students experience the dramatic impact of certain voices connected with historical events, then a recording is the medium to select. If you want to show the correct form of a swimming stroke, a motion picture seems the best choice.

But in many cases more than one medium may be suitable. Your choice may be between preparing a motion picture and making a videotape recording for television use. From the standpoint of the learner, each one provides the necessary visualization of the sequence of events in the same manner. The decision, then, depends on preparation and use factors. Or, in order to treat a stationary subject photographically for individualized learning, the possible media include a photographic print, a slide, a section of a filmstrip, or a microfiche. The question is not which form of still picture representation is *best*, but which is most suitable or acceptable on the basis of such factors as image size and convenience for planned use. Initially one form may be preferred, but when all factors are considered, that may not be the most desirable choice. In making a selection, the following criteria should be considered:

- Does the needed material already exist in suitable form and quality?
- What would the cost of purchase or preparation be?
- What are the reproduction or duplicating costs, if any?
- How much time will be required to locate or prepare each item?
- What are the requirements for equipment, facilities, technical skills, or services in preparation?
- Is one medium more suitable than the others because of ease of viewing or handling by students?
- Will there be problems regarding equipment, facilities, supervision, and scheduling?
- Will there be problems in the maintenance and storage of the materials for future use?
- Do students prefer one kind of material to others?
- What is the teacher's preference?

As you answer these questions, you will find that some materials will rate high on one criterion, moderate on a second, and possibly low on another. If you prepare a chart or a *matrix* like the one illustrated as Table 3, you can quickly see how each medium rates with respect to all criteria and in comparison to the other media.

Table 3. Factors (Criteria) to Consider in Making
Final Media Decision

Criteria	Alternate Materials			
	Photographs	Slides	Filmstrips	Microfiche
Commercially available				
Preparation costs				
Reproduction costs				
Time to prepare				
Skills/Services required				
Viewing and handling				
Maintenance and storage				
Students' preference				
Instructor's preference				

On Table 3, instead of entering general words like *low, moderate, high,* use a three- or five-point numerical rating scale, and assign a number to each box. Then determine which medium has the highest numerical rating by adding up the points. This technique gives a somewhat objective basis on which to make a decision.

This chapter has presented an extensive consideration of two key related elements of the instructional design plan: teaching/learning methods and the supporting instructional resources.

Teacher and student activities and resources are suggested below for our sample topics:

HAIKU

Teacher Activities

1. With a student committee, prepare a dramatic presentation on the history and form of haiku as a slide/tape series. Include participation questions.
2. Using transparencies of traditional and modern haiku, describe the common elements of haiku.
3. Introduce writing assignments by showing slides of subjects on one screen and examples of related haiku on an adjacent screen. Follow up by projecting a subject and asking the students to compose their own haiku on acetate sheets. Have volunteer students then project their poems, pointing out form and use of common elements.

4. Introduce assignment.
5. Visit small groups.
6. Meet with students whose haiku were not acceptable to their groups. Discuss any misunderstandings, and offer new pictures for inspiration.

Student Activities
1. Observe slide/tape presentation. Answer questions on worksheet as they are asked.
2. Observe transparencies presentation. Complete exercises on identifying the elements of haiku.
3. Participate in haiku-writing exercise.
4. Each student will select three pictures from magazines in the library or elsewhere to serve as subjects of haiku.
5. Each student will write a haiku based on each picture. The two the learner considers the best will be evaluated by the small group.
6. Class divides into four groups. Each student shows his or her two pictures and reads the haiku to the small group. On a rating sheet, each student evaluates the work of others in the group as "excellent," "good," or "poor."
7. After conferring with the teacher, students who do not receive a minimum rating of "good" by their groups will form their own group for reevaluation.
8. All students receive a bibliography on haiku and are encouraged to explore the listings and continue writing haiku.

SHEET-METAL CRAFT

Students exploring vocational fields would study this topic for themselves. They can select the activities in any order they wish and skip any activities that do not interest them.

Teacher Activities
1. Meet with student to clarify any information he or she has obtained after completing worksheets and forms. Discuss the student's interest in the subject. At a student's request, make arrangements for the student to visit sheet-metal shops in the community.

Student Activities
1. View 8 mm sound film showing detailed examples of work done by sheet-metal workers. Read printed material that correlates with the film and summarizes the kinds of sheet-metal work.
2. Watch videotaped interviews with representatives of state employment office, sheet-metal workers union, joint apprenticeship committee, and contractors. Complete worksheet on job opportunities and employment advantages.
3. Read printed material describing the required educational background and apprenticeship training program. View 8 mm sound film showing apprenticeship training program. Complete form indicating which required courses you have completed and which you still need.
4. Make appointment to meet with school counselor.
5. Visit one or more sheet-metal shops to observe the work. Talk with the owners and employees.

THE FUTURE

Teacher Activities
1. Introduce the unit by showing the film *Future Shock*. After discussing it, raise questions such as, "What are people who may have insights into the future, writing and saying about the future?" and "How do they arrive at their opinions?"
2. Review unit objectives with students. Divide the class into groups for their investigations. Guide them in selecting topics. Be available for consultation and assistance.
3. Participate in group reporting activities.
4. Assist groups in choosing potential areas of change to study.
5. Be available to offer assistance.
6. Attend final media reports.

Student Activities
1. Participate in discussion after viewing introductory film.
2. Select a topic to investigate, do library research, and prepare a report.
3. Share results with class.
4. Each group should select an area of interest about the future and gather data on current status and future developments from all possible sources—school, community (places and people), industry, and so forth.
5. Prepare a probability report (when anticipated events may happen) including

a time line of future development for the topic investigated.

6. Develop a media presentation as a final report to the group (radio news report, television program, film, or slide series).

OVERHEAD PROJECTION

Student Activities

Objective 1

a. Learn how to use the overhead projector by viewing the videotape demonstration, studying the still photographs displayed in the practice laboratory, reading the manual, or any combination of these activities.

b. Complete the worksheet diagram on projector parts and uses.

c. Practice using the projector in the laboratory with sample transparencies.

Objective 2

a. Develop a rating scale for evaluating transparencies.

b. Compare your scale with those on text page 245; revise or add items to yours if you wish.

c. Choose six transparencies and evaluate them; turn in your evaluations to the instructor.

Objective 3

a. Refer to the assignment sheet on making transparencies. Prepare three kinds, and utilize the various techniques as instructed. Make use of 8 mm films and of the procedures printed in the manual. Ask the lab assistant for help if necessary.

b. Sign up with your discussion group to present your transparencies and demonstrate your competence with the projector.

c. Using the rating scale in the manual, you and the instructor will evaluate the transparencies shown by other students in your group.

d. Students who receive unsatisfactory ratings or low scores on a written exercise, use of a projector, or quality of transparencies, review procedures with instructor and repeat any needed laboratory work. Meet again in a group for evaluation.

Instructor Activities

Participate in objectives 2c, 3c, 3d.

TECHNIQUE FOR WASHING HANDS

Student Activities

1. Read pages 123–126 in the lab manual. Complete exercise on page 127.

2. View the silent 8 mm film *Handwashing Technique*.

3. Review the pictures and descriptions of the technique in the lab manual (pages 127–130).

4. Practice washing your hands in the laboratory.

5. When ready, demonstrate your ability to wash your hands to two other students. Have them grade you on the scale in the manual (page 131). Discuss their findings, and practice your technique again if necessary.

6. When ready, complete the self-check test obtained from the laboratory aide.

Laboratory Aide Activities

1. Be available to assist students as needed.

2. Test each student on technique.

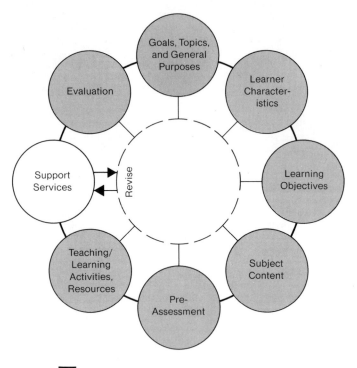

7 *Support Services*

What support services are required to implement the design plan?

In traditional education programs, educators often make plans for using certain instructional methods and for gathering or preparing materials, without considering what support services they will require. These services include funds, facilities, equipment, and personnel whose time must be scheduled for participation in the instructional plan. Teachers and teaching teams frequently neglect to request these necessary services—certain equipment, a particular room, a sum of money, or specific professional or technical assistance—until they are ready to use them. This procedure is not suitable in the instructional design plan, especially because if certain support, like funds or facilities, is not available, it can limit a new planned program severely.

There are many interrelated elements in any instructional situation, and each needs careful consideration during the appropriate planning step. Support services must be considered at the same time instructional plans are being made and materials, being selected. In addition, consideration must be given to coordinating the planned program with other operational aspects of the institution (student schedules, guidance services, and so forth).

This chapter briefly considers all support services, with the exception of matters related to personnel, which are discussed in Chapter Y.

Budget

All new programs require funds to get started. Any school system or other institution interested in supporting innovations in its instructional program must provide money for research and development. After a carefully planned program proves its worth, the returns, in terms of increased learning and better use of teacher services, should justify the initial investment. Financial support may be necessary for any or all of the following:

During Development

Professional planning time
Construction or renovation of required facilities
Purchase of equipment, installation, and checkout on operation
Purchase or preparation of instructional materials, including professional search and planning time, technical staff time, raw materials, and duplicating multiple copies
Development of testing devices for evaluation
Consultative services
Costs of tryouts, including personnel time and consumable materials
Time for planning revisions in the plan and the materials
Time for training teachers and staff for implementation phase
Administrative costs (travel, telephone, overhead, and so forth)

During Implementation

Faculty and staff salaries
Replacement of consumable and damaged materials
Servicing and maintenance of equipment
Depreciation of equipment and overhead charges
Time and materials for updating the program

More attention is given to financial matters in Chapter Z.

Facilities

Facilities for an instructional program may be required for any of the following activities:

- Presentations to groups of regular-size classes (25–30 students) or to large groups (up to many hundreds of students), requiring audiovisual projection, sound amplification, and other features
- Independent study stations (carrels are being used because they seem to reduce noise and to be conducive to studious concentration, but in many programs less expensive open tables are satisfactory) of a suitable size to hold necessary equipment and study materials while still being comfortable for students, plus the necessary electrical outlets, viewing screens, storage areas, and other features
- Small-group meeting rooms with informal arrangements of furniture for teacher-students or student-students interaction, with provisions for audiovisual projection, wall displays (such as chalkboards and exhibits), and other features
- A resource center where materials and equipment are gathered, organized, and made available to instructors and students
- Staff meeting rooms and workrooms

When deciding on facilities for a learning center to serve an individualized-learning program, consider the following four questions:

- How many students are expected in the program?
- How many hours will the average student spend in the learning center?
- How many stations or carrels will be required?
- How many hours will the center be open weekly (possibly with supervision)?

If you know or decide on any three of these factors, you can calculate the fourth. For example:

> 100 students
>
> 4 hours average study time per student in a week
>
> 10 stations

How many hours should the center be open weekly?

$100 \times 4 = 400$ student hours

$400 \div 10 = 40$ hours of use per station

Thus, this learning center should be operated a minimum of 40 hours per week. This assumes continuous, full use of each station. A factor of 10 percent or 20 percent might be added to allow flexibility for repeated use, breakdown of equipment, variations in student schedules, and other unforeseen needs. So, in this problem, 46 to 48 hours of operation would be reasonable. If that makes the hours of operation too long, then the number of stations might be increased.

As the need for specific facilities becomes obvious, consider which existing ones can be used without modification, which ones require minor or major adaptations, and where new construction is essential. Many ideas for adapting present facilities can be obtained by visiting institutions that have similar programs in operation. It may also be necessary to consult with qualified experts who are knowledgeable about space needs for various activities, special equipment and electrical requirements, and other technical matters.

Equipment

When you are deciding upon the kinds of materials to use in a program, be sure also to consider what equipment will be required in order to use them. Is sufficient equipment already available, or must it be obtained? Although decisions about equipment usually depend on your choice of materials, there are instances when the type of equipment available may influence the form of material to be used. For example, still pictures in the form of slides might be preferred for individualized learning, but because filmstrip viewers are available or are much less expensive and easier to use than slide projectors, the planning committee may decide to prepare filmstrips rather than slides.

When you investigate other programs, talk with the technicians, as well as the persons in charge, about the equipment they use. Find out which kinds have proved to be durable and easy to use and which cause the least damage to the materials.

Here, again, expert help may be needed. There is such a wide variety of equipment available today for both group presentations and individual use that it may be difficult to know what to choose without extensive background and up-to-date experience. But do not leave the final decision of equipment to consultants. Those persons involved in a new program should themselves carefully examine and try out whatever equipment is recommended. Have students work with it, also, before you make any final decisions.

Sometimes we are impressed with highly sophisticated, complex equipment that apparently can do many things, some of which we may not need. Often, less complex and less costly equipment can serve equally well. Remember that purchasing equipment may be only the initial expense. The cost of maintenance and the replacement of parts must also be kept in mind. Be practical in requesting what you need, but be reasonable in terms of what funds are available, the complexity of the equipment, and upkeep.

Time and Schedules

Next to personnel, the allocation of time is the most difficult element to deal with in any new program. Finding time to work on the initial planning may be particularly difficult. Often a new program will not be accepted by the administration until some preliminary planning has been completed and a detailed proposal, presented. The time for this preliminary work may have to be borrowed from time that would have been spent on other activities. A real dedication is often required to complete the initial plans.

Time is required for professional planning, for staff and clerical assistance in locating and in preparing materials, for support services for adapting facilities and installing equipment, and for many other things. After the planning is completed, schedules must be set up for trying out the program. During the same period, time must be scheduled for staff orientation and training. Finally, you must draw up the work schedule for teachers, aides, and students in order to put the instructional program into operation.

In an individualized-learning program students must be helped to assume the responsibility for completing their unit assignments within a given time period. For some, it is easy to procrastinate completion or review of materials and retaking tests. If too many students do this, it can bring either administrative problems caused by increased demands as the course nears its end or incomplete grades. So, in scheduling student time, be alert to this important problem and ward it off by setting deadlines for the completion of work and tests.

Coordinating with Other Activities

Too often a new program in a school is treated as if it occupied a world of its own. It may be given preference over regular classes in using facilities, and its participants may seem to have special privileges that other teachers and students in the school know little about and may resent. Coordinating and communicating with others in the building or school system can develop understanding and thus maintain good feelings. Therefore, it is a good plan to explain a new program to all members of a faculty and to keep them advised of the program's progress. Inform them of any activities that may interest them professionally or that may have some influence on them or on their students.

Another group you should maintain contact with is the parents of students participating in the program. If a program is unusual or highly innovative, an orientation meeting should be held for parents. Parents should also be invited to observe the program in operation and be kept informed of its results.

The periodic publication of a brief newsletter can be an effective way to keep administrators, school board, teachers, students, and parents advised of a program and its progress.

Some of the support services for the sample topics are presented below:

HAIKU

Budget: $15 for materials to produce slide/tape series (38 slides and 9-minute recording; 5 additional slides; 4 transparencies; 100 mounted pictures; printed materials)

Personnel: (1) teacher to plan slide/tape series, make presentation, visit small groups, meet with students who need help, review evaluations of students' haiku by groups; (2) 3 students to work with teacher to plan and prepare slide/tape series and to prepare additional slides and transparencies; (3) library aide to find and mount needed pictures

Facilities and Schedules: regular classroom for presentation; 4 small-group areas for two 30-minute periods; library for supplemental reading

Equipment and Materials: synchronous slide/tape unit with slides and recording; overhead projector to show transparencies and student work on acetate; slide projector with 5 slides; 100 mounted pictures; printed materials (worksheets and duplicated sheets of students' haiku)

SHEET-METAL CRAFT

Budget: $750 for materials and services to produce 3 copies of two 8 mm sound films (10 and 6 minutes long), 3 copies of 12-minute videocassette recording, and printed materials

Personnel: (1) vocational counselor to meet with individual students on request; (2) photographer to produce two films (1 month's work); (3) graphic artist to prepare titles and artwork for films (16 hours' work); (4) librarian to gather and assemble information on the craft and to distribute materials to students on request; (5) aide to assist students using equipment in study area

Facilities and Schedules: 3 carrels for intermittent use by students for approximately 30 minutes each; counselor's office for scheduled appointments with students

Equipment and Materials: 2 8 mm sound projectors with 3 copies each of two 8 mm sound films; 1 videocassette recorder with 2 copies of recording; printed materials, such as pamphlets and worksheets on job opportunities, educational requirements, and other needed information

THE FUTURE

Personnel: social-studies and physical sciences teaching team available throughout unit (2 weeks); other teachers to consult as necessary; community resources as required; learning resource center director to provide research assistance; media specialist to assist students with media projects

Facilities: classroom and seminar meeting rooms (2 weeks); learning resources center reference materials on the future, and production laboratory

Equipment and Materials: 16 mm projector and *Future Shock* film on first day; media resources as needed by students

OVERHEAD PROJECTION

Budget: $300 for preparing videotape, for preparing still photographs, for purchasing and preparing practice transparencies, for purchasing commercial transparencies and 8 mm films, and for purchasing materials for student production of transparencies

Personnel: television staff to prepare videotape (3 persons for 8 hours); graphic artist to prepare practice transparencies (12 hours); photographer to prepare display photographs on operation; 2 lab assistants to supervise practice and production lab and assist students (1 week); 2 instructors to meet with ten sections of 20 students each, the following week

Facilities: equipment laboratory and production laboratory (1 week); resource center (to exhibit commercial transparencies for student inspection); two small-group rooms (10 sections for 40- to 50-minute sessions)

Equipment and Materials: 2 videocassette playback machines and copies of videocassettes on projector operation; 6 overhead projectors in practice laboratory with 25 transparencies for practice; 3 8 mm projectors with 8 mm films on the various production techniques; equipment and supplies for producing transparencies; 200 commercial transparencies for evaluations; printed materials (written exercises); 2 overhead projectors in small-group meeting rooms

TECHNIQUE FOR WASHING HANDS

Budget: $75 for purchase of 3 copies of *Handwashing Technique* 8 mm film

Personnel: laboratory aide to supervise practice; instructor for checkout

Facilities: Learning laboratory for 3-day period

Equipment and Materials: 4 sinks in laboratory with soap and towels for 60 students; 3 8 mm silent projectors and 3 copies of the film

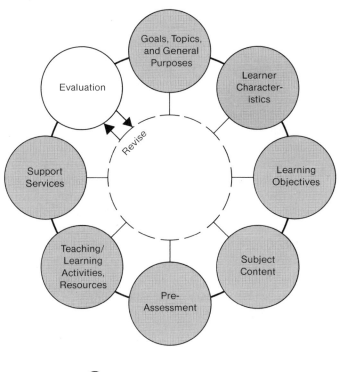

8 *Evaluation*

*How will the amount of student learning
be measured?*

This is the payoff step in your instructional design plan—for
both your students and you. You are ready to measure the learning
outcomes relating to the objectives.

Your objectives indicate what the evaluation should be. By stating them clearly, you have assured measuring directly what you
are teaching. Some authorities even suggest writing the final
examination or designing other evaluation methods first and then
using the individual items of the evaluation as the learning objectives.

At present most teachers prepare a final examination for a topic,
unit, or course as the teaching time draws to a close. The teacher
usually then develops essay or objective questions that refer to the

subject content covered in the course or unit, making little reference to the objectives.

One way to determine whether an instructor is teaching for high-level objectives—applying principles and problem-solving methods in the cognitive area, using tools and operating equipment under the motor-skill performance category or appreciation as an attitudinal objective—is to examine the final examination or other evaluation instrument. If the teacher is really attempting to measure the outcomes specified by the objectives, this will be reflected in the testing.

Once you are satisfied with the extent and completeness of the learning objectives (even though, as Chapter 3 explained, their *final* development may come after later steps in the sequence), you are ready to work on ways to evaluate them. Keep in mind that as you are deciding how to evaluate an objective, it may become clearer to you. Thus, you may still be writing objectives as the program nears completion!

Standards of Achievement

In most conventional educational programs the performance of one student is generally compared to that of other students in the class. This results in a relative rating of each student within the group. The term *grading on the curve* (for example: 10 percent of students receive a grade of *A*, 20 percent get *B*, 50 percent get *C*, and so forth) is often used to describe the way a teacher assigns grades in such a *relative standard* or *normative* fashion. The term *norm-referenced testing* is used to describe this method of reporting achievement. It indicates that one student is more or less proficient, as a result of completing the program, than are other students in the group. This can be important in comparing the accomplishments within one group or class or with respect to local, state, or national norms. But there is no indication of a student's proficiency with respect to levels of subject matter or performance competencies in norm-referenced testing. Therefore, it cannot be assumed that the *A* a student receives in a class this semester is comparable to the *A* another student received in another class taking the same course last semester.

As a result of planning within an instructional design, we intend *each* student to reach a satisfactory level of achievement. Therefore, we need to measure learning outcomes against an *absolute* standard, rather than a relative standard. The standard is the *criterion* specified by the learning objectives. *Criterion-referenced* testing is the measurement of how well each student attains the required level of comprehension and competence specified for each objective pursued. This degree of achievement is independent of the performance of other students. The term *competency-based instruction* is used interchangeably with *criterion-referenced instruction* to identify a program that provides experiences so that most students reach a satisfactory level of proficiency in learning or in performing a task before they go on to the next activity or level.

When criteria are set and students successfully attain them, the concept of *mastery learning* is realized. This is the technique of prompting student success in learning as the proper outcome of an educational program. Its main application at present is for the accomplishment of psychomotor and other technically-oriented objectives. There is concern about the emphasis on mastery learning in some programs because some people fear that, if conventional *ABC* grading is used, each student satisfying the requirements (often through repeated testing until the mastery level is attained) should receive a grade of *A*. Ideally, of course, every student does attain the mastery level, and everyone does get an *A*. As yet, few school or college administrators and parents understand or accept this approach to instruction and grading.

Some advocates of mastery learning recognize mastery, as a *minimum* attainment, which may guarantee a *B* or *C* grade (or possibly a *P* for "pass"). Then higher-level accomplishment (9 or 10 rather than 8 items correct out of 10) or work on optional objectives and activities may be required to attain the *B* or *A* grade. If a number of different performance levels above the minimum acceptable are set, each student is permitted to choose on the basis of his or her capabilities, background, and motivation, what he or she wishes to attempt above the minimum. This procedure is similar to the contract concept used in some schools.

Working with students to help them accomplish their objectives is reflected in criterion-referenced measurement and mastery learning. It fosters cooperation among students, as well. The norm-referenced approach, on the other hand, emphasizes competition.

Paper-and-Pencil Testing

Written tests commonly take either *objective* or *essay* forms. The usual types of objective tests are: true/false, matching, single-word completion, and multiple choice. Most objective tests measure knowledge on the lower cognitive levels, though multiple-choice questions can be used for testing, to some degree, on all levels of the cognitive domain.

Essay tests are more suitable for measuring students' abilities to organize, relate, integrate, and evaluate ideas. They give students flexibility in designing their own responses to a question, thus providing information about how students handle ideas and organize their thinking. Essay tests may ask for a restricted response (an answer relating to a narrow question or a limited situation) or an extended response (an answer permitting the student much freedom in selecting and treating information and defending his or her ideas). In all essay testing, objective methods of grading require rating scales so answers can be judged in terms of conditions, content, and performance of the learning objectives. Objectives to be tested by essay examinations also may have to have these conditions and performance requirements stated more explicitly, so students will know better what is required and how to prepare for the examination. This is another good reason why test questions should be composed right after the learning objectives are written and cross-checked to be certain each objective is being evaluated properly.

For developing questions for paper-and-pencil tests that relate directly to learning objectives, you can obtain help from work that has already been done. First, the taxonomies by Bloom and Krathwohl include sample test items relating to various behavioral levels. Bloom's taxonomy is also the basis of other collections of test items, such as those by Dressel and Nelson, and the Commission on Undergraduate Education in the Biological Sciences. Norris M. Sanders suggests questions that may be asked in the social studies classroom or on tests, again relating to the Bloom taxonomy. (These works are listed in the Bibliography.) In addition, many publications offer assistance in constructing the common types of objective and essay tests.

Evaluating Performance and Psychomotor Objectives

If an objective requires verbal knowledge and other symbol responses (as for the understanding and application of facts, concepts, or principles), then paper-and-pencil tests may be appropriate. But, when an objective includes the term *be able to do* or has other intent for performance, or skill, then measurement methods that are closer to the reality of the objective itself should be used.

Participation in actual situations (driving a car after completing a driver-training program, making a speech as the culmination of a speech course, or judging a film in a film-criticism program) may be the best way to satisfy a performance-type terminal objective.

In some cases, learning activities themselves are the performance. For example, when an objective is "to prepare a leaf collection," the result of making the collection becomes the measure of success. The presentation of a project report to a group can be evaluated as the final outcome of an objective. So, all objectives in a program may not require formal testing.

In cases where an activity itself, a performance, or even a product, is the expected outcome, make sure you establish criteria for judging the acceptability and quality of students' work. A rating scale based on the criteria or on the major elements of a task analysis can provide the objective means of evaluation.

Evaluating Objectives in the Affective Domain

Measuring the attainment of attitudinal and value objectives may require gathering data from students by various means. These means may include observing students' behavior while they are engaged in appropriate activities, listening to their comments, and having them complete questionnaires.

To guide you in gathering data, you might consider developing these tools as appropriate to evaluation needs:

- Observational checklists on student behavior
- Anecdotal records
- Interview questions
- Multiple-choice questionnaires
- Rating scales that include pairs of bipolar adjectives along continuums (interesting–boring, useful–useless)

Testing with Audiovisual and Other Materials

In addition to written tests and actual performances, other testing techniques may be appropriate at times. Sometimes, while an actual performance may be desirable, it may not be realistically possible because of the number of students, the complexity of an operation, cost, or the facilities and time required. In many such cases audiovisual materials can be used as close substitutes. They may even be preferred, since they can concentrate on specific elements of complex situations, as in the examples below:

- Practical manipulation of pictures of objects or materials—for example, from a layout of pictures of tools—require the student either to select the correct ones with which to perform an operation or to show which tools are used with particular materials
- Audio recordings—the identification or analysis of specific voices, descriptions, or situations
- Photographs or slides—the recognition or sequencing of steps in a process; examples or applications
- Films or videotape recordings—identifying correct procedures; reacting to problem situations

Many of these resources are best suited to testing individual students rather than large groups. An individual student may be given the materials to use for a set period of time, during which he or she must respond or perform the required operation. To test larger numbers of students, the instructor can set up a number of stations in a room or laboratory, each one with the equipment or materials for a single problem or question. If there are 20 stations to test 20 students, for example, one student starts at each station. A set number of minutes is permitted for making the response; then the student moves on to the next station. The procedure is repeated until each student has been at each station.

Other testing devices that require students to perform in close-to-reality situations include instructional games, simulation, and role-playing. These three categories do overlap and are often used together in instructional or testing situations.

Consider all these alternatives to the usual paper-and-pencil methods of testing. They can provide realistic measures of objectives. Audiovisual techniques, in particular, can be especially effective with students having low reading ability. Individuals may have different "evaluation-response" styles as they do learning styles, with some students better able to demonstrate their understanding and ability on a visual test than on a written one, for example.

Some Characteristics of Tests

Regardless of whether written, performance, or media-based tests are used, the evaluation phase of an instructional plan should be carefully developed. Some suggestions about evaluations are offered below:

1. Include an evaluation activity for *each* major objective. Sometimes one or more subordinate objectives can also be evaluated with the same test item or activity.
2. An objective that is relatively important may require more than a single test item. This gives students a better chance of demonstrating their proficiency.
3. Make certain each test question directly measures the objective for which it is intended. (This is *item validity*.) If an objective requires the handling or manipulating of objects, use a skill performance measure (or an audiovisual substitute). If the ability to recall information is wanted, then making a list or a short-answer completion item can be appropriate.
4. State test questions clearly, so all students can provide *consistent* responses and their answers reflect their true abilities. (This is *test reliability*.)
5. In determining the efficiency of learning, post-test results often are compared to pretest scores. If this is to be one of the purposes of your program evaluation, be certain the *before* and *after* tests take similar form and treat comparable content.

A number of statistical methods can be used both to judge the suitability of test items and to analyze their results. Refer to standard textbooks on methods of statistical measurement for assistance.

Phases in the Evaluation of Learning

Knowing the results of learning experiences is important both to you and to your students. Therefore, at the end of a learning activity serving one or a series of objectives, plan a brief self-evaluation test for students. Let them check their answers and then review or else discuss with you or an aide any points of difficulty or confusion. This will better assure their preparation for and success in your post-test—especially if mastery learning is your goal.

Self-evaluation is similarly important to the teacher or planning team. You should want to know how well the program you have developed is serving its objectives as it goes along. This is called *formative evaluation,* and it takes place during development and tryouts. It is useful for determining any weaknesses in the instructional plan so you can improve them before full-scale use. Test results, reactions from students, observations of students at work and suggestions from your colleagues may indicate deficiencies in the learning sequence, in procedures, in materials, and so on. For example, the pace of instruction may be too rapid, or too slow or a student may find a sequence uninteresting, confusing, or too difficult.

Formative evaluation also allows the teacher to determine whether, at any point in the instructional sequence, too much previous student knowledge has been assumed or whether the emphasis is on material students already know, so it does not require them to pay much attention.

The procedure of formative, or trial, testing and revision (and possibly retesting and further revision, if necessary) is important to the success of a plan. It should relate not only to the suitability of objectives, subject content, learning methods, and materials, but also to the roles of personnel, the use of facilities and equipment, schedules, and other factors that all together affect the optimum performance for achievement of the objectives. Recall the arrows to/from the various steps in the instructional-design diagram (page 91). They indicate revisions in the plan as the result of evaluation. Remember, the planning process is highly interactive. Each step has effects on the preceding steps, as well as those following. A careful evaluation can reveal shortcomings in one step that require modifications elsewhere.

Sometimes a new program must be implemented without testing the procedures and materials in advance because there is no time or money for doing so. In such a case, the teachers or members of the planning team must rely on their observations of student performances during the first period when the program is in actual use, to determine whether revisions are necessary.

The careful analysis of the results of a program when it is in full use is called a *summative evaluation.* It is concerned with evaluating the degree of students' final achievement of the objectives, as shown by the unit, course, or module post-test. This may also mean following up on students after a course is completed to determine if and how they are using or applying the knowledge, skills, and attitudes treated in the program. At this time you and others may be interested in accountability, in terms of the effectiveness and efficiency of the program. (More attention is given to those matters in Chapter Z.) As in formative evaluation, feedback from summative evaluation should be used for revising and improving any parts of the instructional plan that need it.

Questions you might use in gathering data for formative and summative evaluations are suggested below:

Formative Evaluation (During Tryouts)

1. In terms of the objectives for the unit or module, do students learn at an acceptable level? Where are any weaknesses?
2. Are students able to use the knowledge or perform the skill at an acceptable level? Where are any weaknesses?
3. How long did the learning experience take? Was this acceptable?
4. Did the activities seem appropriate and manageable to the teacher and students?
5. Were the materials convenient and easy to locate, handle, use, file, and so forth?
6. What were the students' reactions to the method of study? to the activities? to the materials used? to the evaluation methods?
7. Do the self-evaluation tests and the post-tests measure the learning objectives?
8. What revisions in the program seem necessary (content, format, and so on)?

Summative Evaluation (During Implementation)

1. To what degree are all objectives achieved?
2. Do students exhibit suitable retention and use of knowledge, skills, and attitudes formed, after a period of time?
3. With large numbers of students, was the use of materials easily managed?
4. Were facilities, schedules, and supervision appropriate to the program?
5. Was there care in handling equipment and materials?
6. Did the materials hold up after repeated use and handling?
7. What are students' attitudes about the subject? the method of study? the activities? their relationships with the instructor and other students?

In both formative and summative evaluations of new, full-course programs, engaging the services of a competent evaluator is recommended. A competent evaluator will know how to devise instruments for measuring students' attitudes and instructors' reactions, and how to analyze the data on learning for each objective. There are also many publications that can assist you in devising your own measuring instruments for cognitive, performance, and attitudinal objectives (see Bibliography).

Evaluation techniques for our sample topics are suggested below:

HAIKU

1. Each student presents his or her two haiku for group evaluation.
2. Students indicate the fundamental elements of haiku they used in their poems.
3. Each student writes a paragraph on the history of haiku, relating haiku to other Japanese verse forms and naming three Japanese haiku poets.
4. Two weeks after the topic is finished, each student describes any haiku writing or reading he or she has done since the topic was concluded.

SHEET-METAL CRAFT

The worksheets completed during student activities will provide much of the factual knowledge related to this craft.

1. The counselor may ask the student to repeat the pretest items, as a measure of factual learning.
2. For the student: What is your reaction to the materials you have studied on the sheet-metal craft, with regard to (a) your interest in the sheet-metal craft as a career and (b) further information you want about the craft?
3. For the student: After you have studied materials on all the trade crafts (plumbing, carpentry, sheet-metal, masonry, and so on), complete a table that indicates for each craft (a) the necessary educational background, (b) training requirements within the craft, (c) length of training period, (d) job opportunities. Then rate your interest in each craft as a possible vocational choice.

THE FUTURE

1. As measured on a rating scale, consensus of class and teacher reactions to the quality and content of the two presentations by each group.
2. Each student writes an answer to this question: "What do you see as the (a) *most desirable* and (b) *least desirable* developments in the world by the year 2000? Give reasons for your choices.

OVERHEAD PROJECTION

Objective 1: Evaluations are made during presentation by each student in the small-group session.

Objective 2: Evaluations prepared by students are reviewed by the instructor.

Objective 3: Transparencies prepared by students are evaluated in group sessions by other students and the instructor, using the accepted rating scale.

TECHNIQUE FOR WASHING HANDS

1. Demonstrate your technique for washing your hands, to your lab aide.
2. Name four routes by which bacteria can be transmitted in a hospital.
3. List three circumstances in a hospital that would necessitate washing your hands.

Part Three

Finally, let us consider some ideas for improving the chances of success of the instructional design plan and some techniques for measuring its outcomes. Part 3 discusses some mechanics that can help in planning, some personnel requirements and working relationships, some ideas for measuring the effectiveness of a plan, and how you might proceed with your own applications of the instructional design plan.

X *The Mechanics of Planning*

Planning for instruction is a complex mental process that requires you to keep many separate elements in mind and to continually reevaluate the relationship of each part of the plan to the whole, because each element affects the development of others. You'll find that insights gained in later planning steps often lead to revisions of earlier steps. Therefore, as you proceed through the sequence of steps, you will find that changes, deletions, and additions will be necessary, making it essential to maintain an open mind throughout the planning process.

One way to begin is to list the topics, purposes, content, and activities for the proposed course of study. The lists can be set down on paper or, if a group is involved in the planning, the items can be written on a chalkboard. Then the lists, on paper, are circulated for comment and revision. However, a list on a sheet of paper or a chalkboard is static, making it difficult to change or add items, which discourages the open-mindedness and flexibility you need in planning.

A better procedure is to make all notations on 4" × 6" index cards. (Cards this size are large enough for most entries and are easy to handle. On the cards, list all details for each step in the plan. Write only one item—an objective, a content fact, an activity, an evaluation item—on each card. Don't worry about the number of cards you use (or throw away). They are inexpensive in terms of the organization of ideas and the use of planning time. Write large, with a fine-tipped felt pen so entries can be seen easily when the cards are displayed.

If possible, use different-colored cards for the different planning categories (at least five colors are available at most stationery stores). For categories that are closely related, such as "topics and general purposes," "learning objectives," and "evaluation," use cards of the same color. For the other categories ("learner characteristics," "subject content," "pre-assessment," "teacher activities," "student activities," and "support services") use cards of different colors. This will enable planners to identify different planning categories at a glance.

By using cards, you make it easy to rearrange, add, and delete items. This gives the flexibility you need in planning. I mentioned earlier that, as you work in one stage of the design plan, ideas may come to mind that will be useful at a later stage. When this happens, jot down those ideas on cards, and set them aside until you are ready to use them.

The cards should be displayed (as described below) so you can see the sequence developing and also so other people can examine your plan. Vertically, a series of objectives develops from simple to complex. Horizontally, you can observe how an objective is handled in terms of subject content, pre-assessment, activities, and evaluation.

One way to display the cards is to lay them out on a table, although loose cards can easily get out of order. Another technique is to tack the cards to a corkboard wall or hold them in place on a magnetic board with small magnets—but in either case it is cumbersome to make changes and add new cards.

The best way to display the cards is to use transparent plastic strips stapled to a board or a wall. The cards are held firmly in the strips (which function as pockets), but they can be slipped in and out easily. Arrange the categories of the design plan horizontally across the board, and place the cards for each category vertically under the appropriate heading. Then it is easy to shift, add, and remove cards until the best sequence is developed. With this arrangement of plastic strips, it is possible to see the development of the plan as it takes shape; when it is completed, the whole plan is visible.

If possible, leave the cards on display so members of the planning team can study the arrangements during their free time. Planning for instruction, like many other creative activities, requires a kind of gestation period for ideas to settle in and to become mature. Therefore, any opportunities for people to look at, study, and think about the entries on the cards and their arrangements may result in worthwhile suggestions for bettering the program. This method of displaying your plans also enables consultants,

Figure 1. Plastic strips stapled to a wall as a planning board for displaying planning cards.

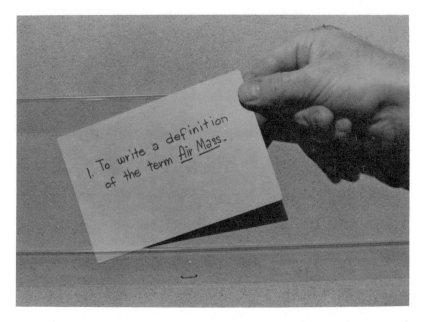

Figure 2. 4″ × 6″ planning card placed behind beaded edge of a plastic strip.

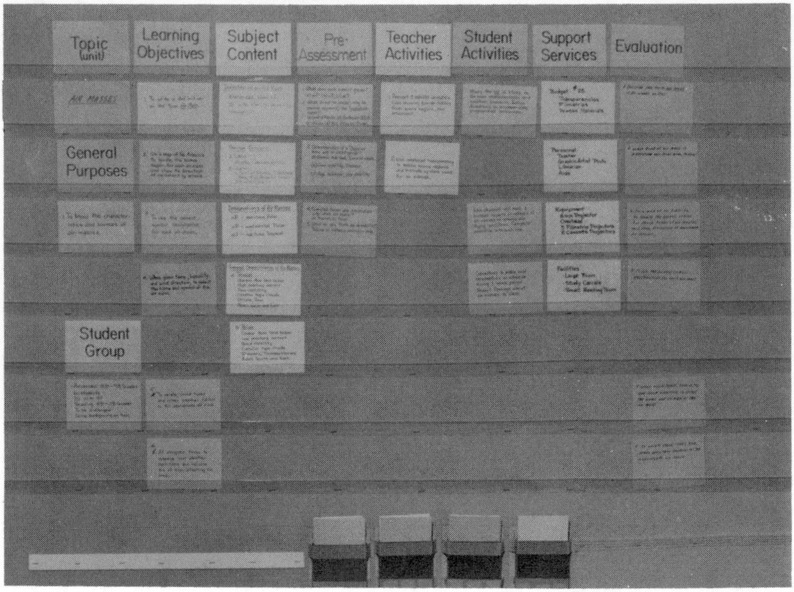

Figure 3. Category headings and entries on cards displayed to illustrate an instructional design plan.

Figure 4. Storyboard sketches as guides for the preparation of slides.

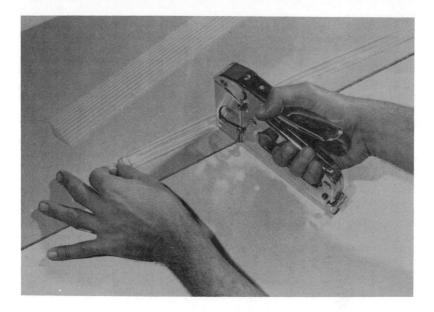

Figure 5. Making a planning board with carpet-runner plastic strips.

administrators, and other interested persons to grasp the intent, extent, and details of the program quickly, even though they have not been involved in the day-to-day planning.

Once the information on the cards reaches final form, the total plan can be transferred to paper and duplicated.

Cards are also good to use in planning the specific details of the learning activities and audiovisual materials. For example, for a slide series, make a sketch of each scene of the series on a card. You can also use cards to diagram the content of a set of transparencies. The layout of these cards on the display board can be studied and evaluated before production is started. This is the storyboarding technique commonly used in planning motion pictures.[1]

Making a Planning Board

The planning board recommended here can be purchased commercially in a small size (2' × 3')[2] or special beaded-edge plastic

---

1. For procedures on planning for the production of audiovisual materials see Jerrold E. Kemp, *Planning and Producing Audiovisual Materials* (New York: T. Y. Crowell, 1975).

2. Medro Educational Products, P.O. Box 8463, Rochester, N.Y. 14618.

strips can be obtained and stapled to a board[3] or you can gather the materials for a board locally and construct it yourself. The plastic strips must have a turned or ribbed edge running horizontally to hold the cards firmly against the wall so they cannot fall through the stapled plastic. Use clear or semitransparent plastic so that writing, placed low on a card, will be visible through the plastic.

Plastic carpet runner, which has a ribbed finish, is one good material for planning-board strips, and you may find others. The board itself can be a section of a corkboard wall. Or a portable board can be made from a heavy-gauge cardboard (14-ply or thicker). (Make it wide enough to hold six to eight columns of cards.) The directions for constructing a planning board are as follows:

1. Cut strips of plastic (1½″ to 2″ wide) the horizontal length of your board, with the ribbing running parallel to the long dimension.
2. Double the plastic over to make a strip ¾″ to 1″ wide.
3. Hold the strip tightly along the board, and attach it with a heavy-duty stapler.
4. Allow about 6″ between strips. Eight strips will make a good-size board.

The matter of using cards for planning and the method of displaying the cards on a plastic-strip board may seem to be minor details, but it is often simple mechanics that determines, to a large measure, whether a new method will be successful or not.

---

3. Chicago Paper Box Company, 5100 Marine Drive, 7A, Chicago, Ill. 60640.

Y *Personnel Capabilities and Working Relationships*

Personnel Capabilities

Professional and technical skills in at least eleven different areas are essential for planning an instructional design and for running a program. It is very likely that some members of any planning team will either have a number of these skills to some degree or be able to acquire them. The broader the abilities of members of a team, the better-qualified the group will be and the less cumbersome will be its size. The responsibilities of the different members of a planning team are listed below. The order of the listing is not an order of importance.

Teacher

The teacher knows the characteristics of the students for whom the instruction is to be designed. He or she must be knowledgeable in the subject area and therefore able to specify the necessary learning objectives and select instructional methods. The teacher should be experienced in using various media in presentations. When the new program is being carried out, the teacher or teaching team has the major responsibility for its success. He or she is now a *director of learning* rather than a disseminator of information, playing an active part in:

- Motivating students to learn
- Working with individual students and groups to select and guide learning experiences

- Monitoring student progress
- Diagnosing difficulties and providing remediation
- Designing evaluation instruments
- Giving praise and encouragement
- Supervising the work of aides

Instructional Designer

The person who holds this job must have had teaching experience and a background in educational philosophy, learning psychology, and instructional methods. This person must be experienced with the instructional design plan and knowledgeable about teaching/learning patterns and instructional resources of all types. He or she must be able to guide the planning process, work with all personnel, and coordinate the program with school administrators. The designer must supervise the scheduled completion of materials, assist in evaluating the tryouts, and help put the program into operation.

Some educators believe instructional designers should be competent in the subject area in which they work. Others feel the instructional designer should have teaching experience, but not necessarily in the content area being planned. That way, the designer may be more objective in guiding the planning. He or she can view the objectives, content, methods, materials, and evaluation methods in a fresh, unbiased way. Because the designer is concerned primarily with the *process* of instructional design, he or she should be able to see the sequencing of objectives without being competent in that subject.

Curriculum and Subject-Matter Expert

The curriculum and subject-matter expert (often the teacher or teaching team) must be competent in the subject in order to be able to suggest content topics, their sequencing, and activities based on the course objectives. This expert must be able to check the accuracy of the subject content and of any instructional materials selected or produced for the program. He or she must be knowledgeable about the relationship of this subject to other subjects in the curriculum and to societal problems. The job requires a person who has a fresh, broad, and imaginative view of the subject and its applications.

Learning Theorist

The learning theorist must have a background in learning psychology. This person's job is to guide the sequencing of learning experiences. Suggesting how to utilize principles of learning (as on page 58), so as to make learning as interesting and effective as possible, is another responsibility of the learning theorist. With suitable qualifications, the teacher, instructional designer, or evaluator might fill this role.

Evaluation Specialist

The job of the evaluator is to assist the professional staff in developing testing instruments for pre-assessing; for knowledge, concept, principle, and peformance testing during the program; and for post-testing. The evaluator will assist in formative testing during program tryouts and in applying the findings for improving the program. He or she may be asked to develop attitudinal and rating scales and to design summative evaluation measures to determine the effectiveness and efficiency of the program. It is strongly recommended that the evaluator be someone from "outside"—having no connection with the program—so the analysis and recommendations will be as objective as possible.

Administrator

The program administrator, a role often filled by the instructional designer, supplies administrative leadership and usually arranges schedules, facilities, personnel assignments, equipment, and budget allocations as the program moves from planning into development and implementation.

Media Specialist

The media specialist must know the advantages and limitations of all kinds of instructional media. This specialist helps select appropriate materials and equipment for each objective. He or she plans, supervises, or carries out the production of all instructional materials made locally, including photographic, graphic, audio, television, programmed, and three-dimensional materials. The media specialist also supervises the preparation of facilities needed in connection with the use of the media. He or she must be able to instruct teachers and students how to use the materials and equipment.

Librarian

The librarian must have a broad knowledge of what is available in order to be able to suggest commercial print and nonprint materials for teaching/learning activities. The librarian is responsible for locating materials as well as for providing services for their use.

Technician

The technician's job is to prepare instructional materials. He or she packages items needed in the program and installs and maintains equipment.

Aides

Aides (sometimes called proctors, facilitators, or miniteachers) assist teachers and others on the staff with semi-instructional and housekeeping tasks, such as preparing materials, supervising laboratory and student-group activities, handling and distributing materials and equipment in the instructional materials center, providing remedial or special assistance to students, and administering and correcting tests. Aides may be graduate students in the subject field, undergraduates who have previously completed the new program, upper-grade students, volunteer parents, or paid professional assistants.

Secretary

The secretary's duty is to handle all office and clerical work, including correspondence, filing, preparing reports, typing, duplicating, and labeling materials.

Students

Increasingly, students are participating in activities that affect them. Many students are intellectually mature and articulate. Their reactions and suggestions to proposed instructional plans can be beneficial. Select two or three students who have already studied the subject, and ask them to participate in planning review sessions. They can react to activities and evaluate unit materials.

The Team

The initial planning team should be small. It may consist of one or more teachers who have subject-content capabilities, an instructional designer who has media-specialist capabilities, and an evaluation expert who has learning-theory capabilities. It is possible that a team of two may possess all the necessary skills. Persons with other abilities should be brought into the program as their services are required.

Working Relationships

A key factor in the success of any instructional planning is the manner in which people work together. In the processes described here, the experiential background and efforts of any member of the team should always be open to review and criticism by other members. This is an unfamiliar method of operation for many educators, and for some it is a challenge to their security and present practices. Some teachers are reluctant to work in this framework. Others have only a casual interest in or motivation for participating in instructional innovation, and need to be helped to face the responsibilities and discipline required.

There are a number of procedures that can help to make a plan work. Members of the planning team should be alert to these procedures when the personnel are being selected, when the planning gets underway, and when the resulting program is implemented. Some of the following statements may seem obvious, and others may repeat ideas presented in earlier chapters, but they are important enough to be stated here.

The instructional designer fills a key role in this plan. Among the designer's major responsibilities are those relating to organizing the planning team and guiding the planning through the steps to implementation. Many of the following suggestions are purposely directed toward the instructional designer as he or she works with faculty members to plan a new instructional program.

The Planning Team

1. If the questions raised in Chapter A are of concern to you, then you should be ready to apply this instructional design plan. Be sure to acquire experience with the plan before attempting to help others apply it. You can begin by selecting a familiar topic and then setting up an instructional design for it, following the plan outlined in this book. Revise and adapt the plan as your situation requires. Also, read some of the publications listed under each heading in the Bibliography. They contain further details and explanations of elements in the instructional design approach.

2. You cannot force instructional change on a teacher or on a team not receptive to change. An instructor who is satisfied with his or her present methods and results is not likely to be interested in changing techniques. The person who is open-minded and concerned about or disturbed at his or her teaching methods, student learning, and student attitudes—the teacher who says, "There must be a better way to teach this material"—is receptive and ready to examine his or her teaching. This person, you can hope, will volunteer to redesign a topic, or a whole course, and will be willing to devote the necessary time and effort to it.

3. The teachers most likely to be interested in this method of instructional planning are those who have already tried and developed innovative techniques such as audiovisual materials or programmed instruction in their own teaching successfully.

4. An instructor who is almost entirely verbally-oriented has more difficulty accepting and understanding the relevance of multi-experience and multimedia approaches to teaching than one who has already tried providing a variety of learning experiences for his or her students.

*5. Get to know the teachers or members of the team with whom you will work. Become acquainted with their philosophies and instructional aims, their approaches to the subject, and

---

*This and all following items preceded by asterisks have been adapted from John Haney, Phil Lange, and John Barson, "The Heuristic Dimension of Instructional Development," *AV Communication Review* Winter 1968, pp. 358–371.

their abilities to select meaningful examples to explain concepts. Visit their classes. Talk with their students. Learn their strengths and weaknesses.

6. See that team members share responsibilities. Do not assign the same person to do research work or reorganize rough notes all the time. Provide clerical assistance when it is needed.

7. Maintain a close liaison among staff members so each one knows what the others are doing and when each one will be called on for work. Have periodic progress reports and evaluation meetings.

8. Teachers, like students, have individual differences. When an instructional plan requiring various teaching/learning methods is being developed for a large number of students, take the interests and abilities of each member of the team into consideration before making specific job assignments. Perhaps one teacher does a fine job in making presentations but does not have the patience for small-group work. That teacher should naturally make presentations and leave interaction sessions to someone who can effectively establish rapport with students and draw them out.

9. When consultants or others are brought in to work with the team, be sure to acquaint them with the project in advance. Inform them of the planning sequence, the present level of accomplishment, problem areas, and other matters they should know about. This will save time and avoid unnecessary discussion or misunderstanding. Be sure to make clear to the consultants what you expect them to do.

Planning Considerations

1. Make sure that the teachers and others on the team realize that planning takes *time* and that it requires much mental work. This should not be pointed out at the beginning, but it should be acknowledged as the team becomes more involved in the project.

2. Develop a schedule, and set time limits for the completion of each phase of the program. If no deadlines are set, it is easy to procrastinate and to work around the big problems.

3. Do not permit planning meetings to last too long. A person's attention span and ability to concentrate drop off after

about two hours. It is better to have shorter, more frequent meetings.

*4. Proceed in the planning on the basis of team agreements, rather than administrative decisions. Each person must establish an open-minded attitude toward questioning and being questioned. There is still more art than science in instructional planning, and as long as this is the case consensus judgments are important. Also, do not hesitate to try more than one approach to a problem and then evaluate each approach objectively.

5. Often, the logical organization of the subject content developed by the instructor or subject expert must be revised as the instructional design—primarily the objectives—is planned. This matter must be approached carefully because an instructor may become upset if someone outside the field questions the organization and thus, indirectly, the instructor's knowledge.

6. In planning, do not work with large blocks of material. Start with a few immediately controllable elements—possibly only one topic or unit. Try them out and, with success, build toward an ultimate course design.

7. The team should recognize that with an instructional design approach finality is never reached. There should be a continuing desire to evaluate results and find better ways to achieve the objectives. This does not mean that a plan is never put into operation. Implement the planning, but be ready at any time to revise it or to make additions that may improve the results.

*8. Don't let words get in the way. Above all, don't use jargon. It can quickly lead to resentment and the loss of cooperation. It is better to learn the instructor's lingo and converse in those terms.

9. Help teachers be *specific* with examples and illustrations. Generalized statements will not suffice when planning learning experiences. Observe the teacher at work. What you see should offer clues for organizing and selecting learning experiences.

*10. Developing objectives is a complex, difficult, and often frustrating experience. Play it by ear. Some instructors can only start with subject-matter lists. Go along with them if necessary. Then gradually lead them to objectives.

11. During planning, play down any emphasis on the mechanics of using equipment for instruction. Audiovisual equipment, as used in traditional classrooms, is sometimes cumbersome, and many teachers don't like to work with it. Therefore, if equipment is needed for the instructional design, make it easy for the teachers to use, perhaps by providing assistants to operate it for them. Students in individualized learning will use new equipment more easily!

*12. Encourage the planning team by arranging visits to successful innovative programs, viewing films that report on new programs, or inviting a person who has been successful in developing a similar program to meet with your teachers. Some teachers find it difficult to imagine how a program that is successful in a field outside their own can be transferred successfully. Help them to see the similarities, and show them how adaptations can be made.

13. Realize that things do not always proceed smoothly and easily in planning. If the planning team runs into obstacles, it is necessary to consider new approaches to achieving your goals.

14. The instructional design plan presented here is a guide, not a formula. Because planning is innovative and requires continuous attention to possible new approaches, the planning process must be flexible. Although each element of a plan needs consideration, the sequence of the planning steps is not fixed. In one situation you may find that one order works best. In another situation, a different approach will be needed.

Relations with Others

1. Keep administrators informed of your progress. The moral and practical support that you and others will need may be easier to obtain when those responsible for a school program know what is being done and what the potential or actual results are.

*2. Encourage administrators to recognize the responsibilities and energies required in planning by providing such incentives or rewards as free time, assistants, reduced teaching loads, opportunities for summer employment to carry out planning, direct financial support for planning, and consideration for promotion.

3. Encourage and provide opportunities for teachers to gain recognition for their efforts by reporting on new programs and their roles in them. The teachers might, for example, write articles for journals and appear at professional meetings to demonstrate the program.

4. Students' acceptance of a new program is influenced by a teacher's attitude. Therefore, be sure that teachers express a positive view toward the plan when they are dealing with students.

5. Explain the plan and its procedures to the students so they will have a clear understanding of their responsibilities.

*6. Involve students in the developmental process. They are the "consumers" of your product, and, as such, they can best judge the interest level, the pacing, and the effectiveness of the learning activities. This enables planners to try out materials and learning experiences on potential student groups and gives students the opportunity to influence the results.

7. If the program will bring about a major change in school procedures, be sure to inform parents about the nature of the program in the beginning. Then keep them informed of its progress.

8. Anticipate criticism. Your efforts will probably have to stand up to the scrutiny of your colleagues. They may find fault with your instructional-design plan. Their own lesson plans cannot be questioned in the way an instructional design can because they lack specificity and definite direction.

9. It is inevitable that in many institutions—public school systems as well as colleges and universities—systematic plans and support for instructional development will be established. This will come about most likely as academic leaders or curriculum committees recognize the value of coordinating all services relating to instruction (library, audiovisual, television, computer, testing, and so forth) and providing for the instructional designer role described here.[1]

---

1. For a report on the systematic establishment of an educational development program in one institution, see John E. Dietrich and F. Craig Johnson, "A Catalytic Agent for Innovation in Higher Education," *Educational Record* Summer 1967, pp. 206–213.

Z Measuring the Outcomes of the Plan

Parents, administrators, school boards, legislators, and the general public—often through their votes and other decisions—keep asking, "What are we getting for our money?" An important second question is, "Are the results worth it?" The interest in the *accountability* of eductors reflects these concerns and requires us to find satisfactory answers for these questions.

Education is one of the few enterprises in the country for which almost no cost-effectiveness studies have been made. Admittedly, in educational programs there are many complex variables that would have to be considered. A number of them are not measurable or else require study of long-term results (for example, increased earning power of the students after they become adults, decreased welfare expenditures, decreased losses to the community from criminal acts). An absolute measure of the ultimate outcomes of an educational program is beyond us at this time. But we can draw some valid conclusions about a new program that can permit us—and the control agencies—to make some judgments about its immediate value.

This matter of examining program outcomes relates to summative evaluation, considered in Chapter 8 as part of the evaluation element of your instructional design plan. The question you must answer is; "How effective and efficient has the program been in achieving the desired objectives for the student group?"

Effectiveness

Begin your evaluation by asking yourself, "How well did the students do?" To find the answer, determine how many students

119

accomplished the stated objectives for a unit, module, or course within the time set. Or, to be more specific, you should determine the percentage of students who reached an acceptable level of achievement for each objective. This information should be a matter of record, ascertained from test scores, ratings of projects and performance, and records of observations of students' behavior. It can easily be presented in a table or chart. The data can be interpreted as a measure of the *effectiveness* of the instructional design plan for this group of students.

For example, if *all* students accomplished *all* objectives, the effectiveness of the program was excellent. If 90 percent of the students accomplished all objectives, or if 90 percent satisfactorily completed 86 percent of the objectives, has the program been efficient? To answer this, faculty and administration must decide on what level to accept the program as effective.

Realistically, it is very likely that because of individual differences among students and your inability to design ideal learning experiences, you cannot hope to reach the absolute standard of 100 percent, but must settle for a somewhat lower level of accomplishment. Then another question must be answered. Assume that your performance standard requires all students to accomplish 90 percent of the objectives, but they actually accomplish 86 percent of them. What time, effort, and expense are required to redesign the weak areas of the program in order to raise the learning level to 90 percent? Is the effort to reach the 90 percent level worth the cost? There may be factors that would make the cost of achieving your goals almost prohibitive. You may have to settle for a somewhat lower level of accomplishment until someone develops a revision of the program that will make it possible to reach the desired level of performance with reasonable effort.

Criteria other than the students' achievement of unit or course objectives are important for judging the effectiveness of a program also. From a list prepared by Robert M. Diamond, the following can be selected as useful indicators:[1]

Student: Improved learning, same cost; equal learning, less cost; reduced failure rate; improvement in attitudes (toward sub-

---

1. Robert M. Diamond and others, *Instructional Development for Individualized Learning in Higher Education* (Englewood Cliffs, N.J.: Educational Technology Press, 1975), p. 114.

ject, education, institution, society); less time required; and increase in student credit points

Faculty: Increase in faculty student ratio (reduction of teacher-cost per student); less instruction time required; increased opportunities for specialization and subject offerings; increased direct student contact (no increase in cost); and improvement in attitudes of faculty (toward students, course, department, institution)

Space: Less required; more students accommodated

Resources: Increase in total utilization; increase in efficiency of use (units reach more students)

Community: Improved attitude toward institution; more community needs being met

Efficiency

In evaluating *efficiency*, two aspects of a program require attention. One is a measurement of *student performance*, principally in individualized learning programs. This measurement is the ratio of the number of objectives a student achieves to the time the student takes to achieve them. For example, Bill satisfies 7 objectives in 4.2 hours of study and work. By dividing the number of objectives Bill achieves by the amount of time it takes him to accomplish them, we find that his performance index is 1.7 (7 ÷ 4.2). Mary achieves the 7 objectives in 5.4 hours. Her performance index is therefore 1.3. Thus, the *higher the index*, the *more efficient* the student's performance. The index may be calculated on a class basis, and the information can be useful in evaluating the efficiency both of the students and of the activities and resources in the instructional design plan. Subjective decisions must be made for accepting the level of a performance index or the need to raise the index through revision of activities and materials.

Cost

The other aspect of efficiency is *cost*. Before you can assess the efficiency of a program, you must determine how much it costs per student in order to reach the accepted effectiveness level. This cost per student can be called the *instructional cost index*. To determine it, it is necessary to tabulate all factors that are chargeable to the design plan for the instruction given to a particular student group. This cost structure should consist of two parts: (1) *developmental costs* of planning and pilot tryouts and (2) *operational costs* incurred during actual implementation.

The developmental costs could be relatively high and should be considered separately from the ongoing operational costs of a program. Once calculated, the developmental costs should be amortized over a period of time. This means that a portion of the developmental costs (for example, one-fifth of the total amount for each of five semesters or school years) is added to the operational cost. The *instructional cost index* for any semester is calculated by dividing the sum of the operational cost total and the proportion of the developmental cost total by the number of students satisfactorily completing the work.

The *developmental costs* include:

- Planning time (percentage of salary for time spent by each member of the planning team on the project, or number of hours spent by each member multiplied by his or her hourly salary rate, and fees for consultants)
- Staff time (percentage of salary for time spent by each member engaged in planning and production and in gathering materials, or the number of hours spent by each person multiplied by his or her hourly salary rate)
- Supplies and materials
- Outside services for preparing or purchasing materials
- Construction or renovation of facilities
- Equipment
- Installation of equipment
- Testing, evaluation, redesign, reproduction, and so on of resources (including personnel time and costs of materials and services)
- In-service education for teachers, aides, and others who will participate in the program during implementation (cost for time)
- Overhead (utilities, furniture, room or building costs or depreciation allowance)
- Miscellaneous (office supplies, telephone, travel, and other items)

The *operating costs* include:

- Administrative salaries (based on percentage of time) chargeable to the project
- Faculty salaries for the time spent in the program working with groups and individual students, planning daily activities, evaluating program, revising activities and materials
- Salaries for aides, maintenance technicians, and others
- Replacement of consumable and damaged materials
- Repair of damaged equipment
- Depreciation of equipment
- Overhead for utilities, facilities, furnishings, custodial services
- Evaluating and updating materials (time and materials)

To determine an instruction cost index, first total the dollar amount for all factors listed as developmental costs. Then divide this sum by the number of years over which the developmental costs are to be amortized. Next, total the costs for the operational phase. To this amount add the prorated developmental cost, and divide the final total by the number of students in the program (the number of students may vary from one semester to the next). The result is the instructional cost index.

Here is an example of the calculations for an instructional cost index:

Developmental Costs

Planning time:
3 people (2 teachers and 1 designer-media specialist),
2 weeks summer @ $600 .... $1,800

Staff time:
librarian, 1 week summer .... $ 300
graphic artist/photographer, 120 hours @ $6 720
secretary, 2 weeks @ $100 200
student assistants, 100 hours @ $2.50 250
                                                      $1,470

Supplies and materials:
graphics/photo .... $ 200
audio tape cassettes 60
printing guides 100
                                                      $ 360

Outside services:

film processing and duplication	$ 250
commercial filmstrips	80
library books and microfilms	225
laboratory supplies	300
	$ 855

Renovating facilities:

constructing carrels in lab	$ 300

Equipment:

10 8 mm projectors @ $130	$1,300
10 cassette tape recorders @ $50	500
10 filmstrip viewers @ $40	400
1 microfilm reader	250
	$2,450

Testing and redesign (no professional time charged)

staff time, 30 hours @ $6	$ 180
materials	50
	$ 230

In-service education:

3 lab assistants, 10 hours @ $3	$ 90

Overhead:

planning and production facilities	$ 200

Miscellaneous:

office supplies, car travel	$ 100

Total Development Cost $7,855

Operating Costs (One Semester)

Administrative salaries:

1 teacher, 0.10 time @ $12,000	$1,200

Faculty salaries:

2 teachers, 0.20 time @ $12,000	4,800
	Total $6,000

Staff salaries:

lab assistants, aides, technicians, 300 hours @ $4	$1,200
librarian, 0.10 time @ $10,000	1,000
	Total $2,200

Replacements	$ 200
Repair	100
Overhead	500
Updating materials:	
40 hours labor @ $6	$ 240
materials	40
	Total $1,080

Total operational costs	$ 9,280
Portion of developmental cost (0.20)	1,571
	Final total $10,851

Number of students in program: 116
Instructional cost index: $93.54

If this program continues beyond five semesters (at which time all developmental costs will have been amortized) and the number of students remains the same, the instructional cost index will then drop to $80. During this period limited funds are included for minor updating and revision of the materials. At the end of five semesters a reexamination of the program for this course may be advisable. Then new developmental costs—we hope, lower than the original ones—would be required. These would affect the on-going operational cost index.

There are other, more comprehensive ways of calculating cost-effectiveness, that weigh various elements and include other factors. But this method is sufficient to give a fair approximation of the instructional cost per student.

The index number itself has no meaning. Calculations could also be made in the same way for traditional program costs in a comparable subject area. But it is difficult (and usually unfair) to make a comparison between a new program with carefully structured objectives and a traditional program based on generalized objectives. It would seem more appropriate to compare a unit of study for two math classes, a biology and a chemistry course, or third- and fourth-grade social studies classes if they have been systematically planned and implemented.

After the costs for a number of different topics, units, or whole courses have been assessed, it would be possible then to determine whether operating costs for a particular topic are too high, acceptable, or relatively low. The calculations should be repeated each time a particular unit or course is taught, so any change in the cost index can be determined and the reasons for the change evaluated.

If a program proves to be effective in serving students' needs (and it should be constantly evaluated and revised until it does) but the instructional cost index remains higher than desired, certain steps might be taken to lower the index, as follows:

- Include more students in the program. This will increase the denominator of the formula.
- Decide if there are any activities for which teacher's aides might replace teachers *without reducing the effectiveness of the program.*
- Plan to relieve teachers of some student-contact time by developing additional independent study activities for students.
- As a last resort, lower some of the required performance levels.

Subjective Measures of Outcomes

To this point, we have been examining quantitative, analytical ways of evaluating a new program. This approach may seem too materialistic and impersonal when dealing with humans. Let us recognize that there are many nonquantitative outcomes of an instructional program also. Just as we recognized the elusive, difficult-to-measure objectives in the affective domain, so we should understand that subjective evaluations of the effectiveness of an instructional program are also possible. Observations of the behavior of students and replies to the informational and attitudinal questionnaires and rating scales by students, teachers, and staff at the end of a unit or at the conclusion of a course may indicate the degree of success for the various phases of a program.

Also, you might consider follow-up studies of students—their study habits next term (for example, their ability to work independently, if this has been a part of the program), their accomplishments in subsequent courses, their future selection of courses and vocational or avocational interests that may possibly have been motivated by their achievements in the program. These are some ways to make subjective judgments of the success of your instructional design plan.

Now What . . . ?

Most often when people finish studying a book, participating in a workshop or seminar, or taking a course, they heave a sigh of relief (whatever that indicates!) or possibly they thank the instructor, telling him or her how much they "enjoyed" the program . . . and then turn to other important matters. We can hope they acquired some insights, knowledge, and skills they could use.

What about your response to this book and the course of which it is a part? Do you find your reaction listed below?

- The ideas presented here are good, but who has time to do all this planning for a course?
- I'd like to develop a plan for individualized learning at my school, but neither my department chairman nor the principal is in favor of such an approach to teaching.
- If I wanted to try a new program, where could I find the money for equipment and materials? My district is broke.
- You've given me some help in my thinking about teaching, but I'm not really interested in doing anything different at this time . . . maybe sometime later.
- Boy, is this great! I'm going to get teachers in my school right into instructional design. This is the *only* way to plan instruction.
- I'm glad the course is over and I have my three units of credit.
- I like this method of planning. I'm going to try it.
- I'm already doing much of this in my planning. Now I see how I might more easily work on higher intellectual and attitudinal objectives with my students.

Many of these statements indicate some level of readiness or willingness on your part to move toward implementing instructional change. Others indicate a hesitancy or lack of interest in the ideas presented here. I respect this attitude.

If you are ready, Chapter Y offers you a number of planning considerations. You may want to review them. Here are some additional suggestions for proceeding:

1. Start small. Extend what you started as a project in the course (if you used the study guide that accompanies this book). Try it out with students. The learning outcomes should be successful. Revise your planning as necessary. Then develop another topic in your program, and so on.

2. Feel free to modify, or even simplify, the procedures presented here. Maybe you will start by only treating the objectives, the activities/resources, and the evaluation elements of your instructional design plan. Get assistance from an instructional designer or someone else who has been successfully doing some planning. Such a person, who can objectively react to your plans, can be helpful.

3. Talk over your ideas and plans with your administrator. Show the administrator the planning for your course project. Get his or her understanding and support (if possible, get it in action as well as in words) for such things as free time, budget, facilities, or whatever you need as a minimum to get started.

4. Even if your immediate supervisor or administrator is not receptive to your plans, don't be deterred. You can still move ahead. Look to other positive support services in your district or institution, such as instructional development services and media staff. When you are ready, have the administrator see your program in operation. Show the learning results—the effectiveness. Inform parents, and enlist their support.

5. After you have some preliminary experience and results, try to involve your colleagues, so they can share the development efforts. If two or three teachers work together with an instructional designer, they can prepare a full course in a reasonable period of time.

6. Mature students in your classes can be very helpful in reacting to your plans, in gathering materials for your units, and in trying out the plan. With success, they can be excellent emissaries to other teachers.

7. Don't be upset if most of your colleagues do not react favorably to your planning approach and your enthusiasm.

8. Somewhere down the road, report the success of your program to other educators, parents, the school board, and even legislators. Use a dynamic visual form, possibly a multiscreen slide/tape. We all need to see and hear about systematically planned, effective, and efficient programs.

9. Finally, ask yourself this important question: "What's in it for me?" If you can answer it in a positive "affective-domain" way, and if instructional design planning can be a *priority* activity in your professional life . . . you'll be on your way.

GOOD LUCK.

Appendix

The five topics selected to illustrate the eight steps of the instructional design plan are presented here in their entirety. Remember, they are examples and may not be complete treatments of actual units or modules. The arrangement of elements in the plan for each example simulates the horizontal and vertical layout of cards on a planning board.

Example 1

GENERAL PURPOSE	LEARNER CHARACTERISTICS
To develop an appreciation for haiku by writing it	Average Grade 8 class, 35 students
	IQ, 96–128
	Reading levels, Grades 6–12
	The topic of haiku was considered for class study after much interest was shown in a student's report on Japanese literature.
	Students are capable of taking responsibility for independent projects. They enjoy sharing materials in small groups.

EXAMPLE 1. HAIKU   133

LEARNING OBJECTIVES	SUBJECT CONTENT

1. To describe the history and form of haiku, with reference to at least three other forms of Japanese poetry and three historical poets. *Justification:* This will provide you with a background for understanding and appreciating this form of poetry.
2. To apply the three elements commonly used for description in haiku by writing a haiku on two pictorial subjects, each of which is rated at least "good" by a majority of the class on a rating scale *(terminal objective).* *Justification:* The best way to learn about haiku is to write some yourself.
3. To express a positive interest in haiku as a form of literature *(terminal objective).* *Justification:* This will indicate your appreciation of haiku.

History of Haiku

1. Forms of Japanese poetry
   a. *tanka,* 31 syllables in five lines (5-7-5-7-7)
   b. *choka,* poems longer than five lines
   c. *sedoka,* special development of six lines
   d. *renga,* three or more poems making up link-verse sequences
   e. *haiku,* first three lines of tanka or renga
2. Historical Poets
   a. Matsuo Basho (1644–1694), greatest of the haiku poets, wrote his reactions to nature.
   b. Yosa Buson (1716–1784) wrote of the warmth of human affairs.
   c. Kobayashi Issa (1763–1828) emphasized the lives of the common people.
   d. Setchuan Jakushi (1848–1908) brought a modern approach to haiku composition.

Form of haiku

1. First line, 5 syllables
2. Second line, 7 syllables
3. Third line, 5 syllables

Elements Common to Most Haiku

1. Refers to seasons of the year
2. Implies a relationship of human beings and nature
3. Expects the reader to feel the scene described, as something personal

PRE-ASSESSMENT

Prerequisite Quiz

1. From your past experience with poetry tell whether the following sentences are true or false.
   a. In proper poetic form, the final two lines of a poem should rhyme.
   b. All lines in a poem contain the same number of syllables.
   c. Poetry is a method of expression found in the cultures of most countries.
   d. There are many different forms of poetry.

Pretest Questions

2. What country did the haiku verse form originate in?
   a. India
   b. China
   c. Japan
   d. Vietnam
3. Write the correct syllable form for haiku.
4. Which of the following are characteristic of most haiku?
   a. Treats a subject humorously
   b. Deals with the relationship between man and nature
   c. Deals with war and human suffering
   d. Identifies a season of th year.
5. Have you ever written your own haiku?

   Note: For students who answer Questions 2, 3 and 4 correctly, Teacher Activity 2 may be optional.

ACTIVITIES AND RESOURCES

Teacher Activities

1. With a student committee, prepare a dramatic presentation on the history and form of haiku as a slide/tape series. Include participation questions.
2. Using transparencies of traditional and modern haiku, describe the common elements of haiku.
3. Introduce writing assignments by showing slides of subjects on one screen and examples of related haiku on an adjacent screen. Follow up by projecting a subject and asking the students to compose their own haiku on acetate sheets. Have volunteer students then project their poems, pointing out form and use of common elements.
4. Introduce assignment.
5. Visit small groups.
6. Meet with students whose haiku were not acceptable to their groups. Discuss any misunderstandings, and offer new pictures for inspiration.

Student Activities

1. Observe slide/tape presentation. Answer questions on worksheet as they are asked.
2. Observe transparencies presentation. Complete exercises on identifying the elements of haiku.
3. Participate in haiku-writing exercise.
4. Each student will select three pictures from magazines in the library or elsewhere to serve as subjects of haiku.
5. Each student will write a haiku based on each picture. The two the learner considers the best will be evaluated by the small group.
6. The class divides into four groups. Each student shows his or her two pictures and reads the haiku to the small group. On a rating sheet, each student evaluates the work of others in the group as "excellent," "good," or "poor."
7. After conferring with the teacher, students who do not receive a minimum rating of "good" by their group will form their own group for reevaluation.
8. All students receive a bibliography on haiku and are encouraged to explore the listings and continue writing haiku.

EXAMPLE 1. HAIKU 135

SUPPORT SERVICES

Budget: $15 for materials to produce slide/tape series (38 slides and 9-minute recording; 5 additional slides; 4 transparencies; 100 mounted pictures; printed materials)

Personnel: (1) teacher to plan slide/tape series, make presentation, visit small groups, meet with students who need help, review evaluations of students' haiku by groups; (2) 3 students to work with teacher to plan and prepare slide/tape series and to prepare additional slides and transparencies; (3) library aide to find and mount needed pictures

Facilities and Schedules: regular classroom for presentation; 4 small-group areas for two 30-minute periods; library for supplemental reading

Equipment and Materials: synchronous slide/tape unit with slides and recording; overhead projector to show transparencies and student work on acetate; slide projector with 5 slides; 100 mounted pictures; printed materials (worksheets and duplicated sheets of students' haiku)

EVALUATION

1. Each student presents his or her two haiku for group evaluation.
2. Students indicate the fundamental elements of haiku they used in their poems.
3. Each student writes a paragraph on the history of haiku, relating haiku to other Japanese verse forms and naming three Japanese haiku poets.
4. Two weeks after the topic is finished, each student describes any haiku writing or reading he or she has done since the topic was concluded.

Example 2

GENERAL PURPOSE	LEARNER CHARACTERISTICS
To motivate an interest in sheet-metal craft as a vocation (This self-instructional topic is available to students as they explore various vocational possibilities. It should be correlated with similar topics for other crafts.)	Any interested high school student Generally below median socioeconomic background IQ, 95–112 Reading level, average or below grade Most do not expect to go to college. Some need challenges to keep them in school.

EXAMPLE 2. SHEET-METAL CRAFT   137

LEARNING OBJECTIVES	SUBJECT CONTENT
1. To acquire information about the sheet-metal craft as a possible vocational choice *(terminal objective).* *Justification:* In order to examine this trade, you need the information that you can learn from achieving the following objectives. 　a. To describe four kinds of work done by sheet-metal craftspeople 　b. To identify five types of job opportunities and at least three employment advantages in the craft 　c. To list all educational courses and training required for entering the craft 2. To compare your interest in the sheet-metal craft with your interest in other crafts *(terminal objective)* *Justification:* With the information you have learned, you can make some assessment of your interest in and qualifications for this craft.	**Kinds of Sheet-Metal Work** 1. Planning, layout, fabrication, assembly, and installation of metal products 　a. Surfaces 　b. Interior furnishings 　c. Exteriors of buildings 　d. Ducts 2. Determining sizes and types of metal or other materials 3. Using a variety of tools to cut and form metal 4. Performing cutting, forming, and other operations **Employment opportunities** 1. Fabrication plants 2. Custom-work shops 3. Installation contractors 4. Government agencies 5. Heavy industry 6. Self-employment **Monetary advantages** 1. Good hourly wage scale 2. Paid vacations, health and welfare funds, and pensions **Possible future advancement** 1. Growing field of employment 2. Advancement to detailer or estimator 3. Further advancement to foreman, superintendent, or contractor 4. Self-employment **Recommended educational background** 1. High school diploma (required) 2. Several semesters of math, including fractions and decimals, geometry, and trigonometry 3. Industrial arts **Apprenticeship (4 to 5 years)** 1. Some individuals can acquire the skills of the trade through correspondence and trade school courses or by learning from an experienced craftsman, but the usual way is to enter a formal apprenticeship program.

PRE-ASSESSMENT	ACTIVITIES AND RESOURCES

Because the purpose of this topic is motivational and informational, the pre-assessment should measure what the student already knows about it, and serve to interest him or her in it.

1. In which two of the following projects would a sheet-metal craftsperson work?
   a. Riveting the steel frame of a high-rise structure
   b. Making a church spire out of aluminum
   c. Building a plastic hull for a boat
   d. Constructing the ducts for an air-conditioning unit.
2. Which of these tools are used in sheet-metal work?
   stripper
   pipe wrench
   sander
   pipe threader
   snips
   oscilloscope
   air brush
   jointer
   hammer and anvil
   power shears
3. Which statement(s) are true of the sheet-metal craft?
   a. A high school diploma is required.
   b. Apprenticeship is 6 to 8 years.
   c. You can become a journeyman after a successful apprenticeship.
   d. Welding and soldering are two metal-sealing operations.
   e. The joint apprenticeship committee in a community provides on-the-job experiences for individuals.

Students exploring vocational fields would study this topic for themselves. They can select the activities in any order they wish and skip any activities that do not interest them.

Teacher Activities
Meet with student to clarify any information he or she has obtained after completing worksheets and forms. Discuss the student's interest in the subject. At a student's request, make arrangements for the student to visit sheet-metal shops in the community.

Student Activities
1. View 8 mm sound film showing detailed examples of work done by sheet-metal workers. Read printed material that correlates with the film and summarizes the kinds of sheet-metal work.
2. Watch videotaped interviews with representatives of state employment office, sheet-metal workers union, joint apprenticeship committee, and contractors. Complete worksheet on job opportunities and employment advantages.
3. Read printed material describing the required educational background and apprenticeship training program. View 8 mm sound film showing apprenticeship training program. Complete form indicating which required courses you have completed and which you still need.
4. Make appointment to meet with school counselor.
5. Visit one or more sheet-metal shops to observe the work. Talk with the owners and employees.

EXAMPLE 2. SHEET-METAL CRAFT   139

SUPPORT SERVICES

Budget: $750 for materials and services to produce 3 copies of two 8 mm sound films (10 and 6 minutes long), 3 copies of 12-minute videocassette recording, and printed materials

Personnel: (1) vocational counselor to meet with individual students on request; (2) photographer to produce 2 films (1 month's work); (3) graphic artist to prepare titles and artwork for films (16 hours' work); (4) librarian to gather and assemble information on the craft and to distribute materials to students on request; (5) aide to assist students using equipment in study area

Facilities and Schedules: 3 carrels for intermittent use by students for approximately 30 minutes each; counselor's office for scheduled appointments with students

Equipment and Materials: 2 8 mm sound projectors with 3 copies each of 2 8 mm sound films; 1 videocassette recorder with 2 copies of recording; printed materials, such as pamphlets and worksheets on job opportunities, educational requirements, and other needed information

EVALUATION

The worksheets completed during student activities will provide much of the factual knowledge related to this craft.

1. The counselor may ask the student to repeat the pretest items, as a measure of factual learning.

2. For the student: What is your reaction to the materials you have studied on the sheet-metal craft, with regard to (a) your interest in the sheet-metal craft as a career and (b) further information you want about the craft?

3. For the student: After you have studied materials on all the trade crafts (plumbing, carpentry, sheet-metal, masonry, and so on), complete a table that indicates for each craft (a) the necessary educational background, (b) training requirements within the craft, (c) length of training period, (d) job opportunities. Then rate your interest in each craft as a possible vocational choice.

Example 3

GENERAL PURPOSE	STUDENT CHARACTERISTICS
To help students consider the world of the future and its possible effects on their lives	30 advanced students, Grades 11 and 12
	In the upper quartile intellectually
	Reading ability, Grades 10–14
	Mature enough to engage in inquiry experiences
	The previous unit examined historical predictions about the present.

EXAMPLE 3. THE FUTURE   141

LEARNING OBJECTIVES	SUBJECT CONTENT
1. Identify what significant people are writing about the future. 2. Describe how those people arrived at their opinions. 3. Select one social or scientific area, and predict in detail how it will change or develop by the year 2000, and then describe the possible effects of the change upon you as an individual *(terminal objective)*. *Justification:* After examining what specialists say about the future, you should be able to make an educated guess about one aspect of the future and its influence on your life.	1. Major writings on the future Daniel Bell, *Toward the World 2000* Arthur Clarke, *Profiles of the Future* Don Fabun, *Dynamics of Change* Robert Heilbroner, *The Future as History* Herman Kahn, *Thinking About the Unthinkable* Herman Kahn and Anthony Weiner, *The Year 2000* John McHale, *The Future of the Future* Dennis Meadows, *The Limits of Growth* Gordon Taylor, *The Biological Time Bomb* Alvin Toffler, *Future Shock* 2. Possible areas of future change or development Behavior modification Land use Medical priorities Weather control Priorities in society Cities Politics tomorrow War and violence Use of outer space Transportation Communications Shelter

PRE-ASSESSMENT	ACTIVITIES AND RESOURCES
No formal testing or questioning is planned.	**Teacher Activities** 1. Introduce the unit by showing the film *Future Shock.* After discussing it, raise questions such as, "What are people who may have insights into the future, writing and saying about the future?" and "How do they arrive at their opinions?" 2. Review unit objectives with students. Divide the class into groups for their investigations. Guide them in selecting topics. Be available for consultation and assistance. 3. Participate in group reporting activities. 4. Assist groups in choosing potential areas of change to study. 5. Be available to offer assistance. 6. Attend final media reports. **Student Activities** 1. Participate in discussion after viewing introductory film. 2. Select a topic to investigate, do library research, and prepare a report. 3. Share results with class. 4. Each group should select an area of interest about the future and gather data on current status and future developments from all possible sources—school, community (places and people), industry, and so forth. 5. Prepare a probability report, (when anticipated events may happen) including a time line of future development for the topic investigated. 6. Develop a media presentation as a final report to the group (radio news report, television program, film, or slide series).

EXAMPLE 3. THE FUTURE   143

SUPPORT SERVICES	EVALUATION
Personnel: social-studies and physical sciences teaching team available throughout unit (2 weeks); other teachers to consult as necessary; community resources as required; learning resource center director to provide research assistance; media specialist to assist students with media projects Facilities: classroom and seminar meeting rooms (2 weeks); learning resources center reference materials on the future, and production laboratory Equipment and Materials: 16 mm projector and *Future Shock* film on first day; media resources as needed by students	1. As measured on a rating scale, consensus of class and teacher reactions to the quality and content of the two presentations by each group. 2. Each student writes an answer to this question: "What do you see as the (a) most desirable and (b) least desirable developments in the world by the year 2000? Give reasons for your choices.

Example 4

Subject Area: Instructional Technology
Unit: Projected Audiovisual Materials and Equipment
Topic: Overhead Projection

GENERAL PURPOSE	LEARNER CHARACTERISTICS
To be prepared for using the overhead projector in teaching	200 elementary teacher-education students
	This unit is studied the semester before student teaching
	Some students have used the overhead projector a little; all have seen it used in classes.
	Many profess having only limited mechanical ability.

EXAMPLE 4. OVERHEAD PROJECTION   145

LEARNING OBJECTIVES	SUBJECT CONTENT

1. To operate the overhead projector with a rating of at least 9 on a 10-point scale *(terminal objective)*.
  a. To set the projector in proper position for use
  b. To locate the three main controls
  c. To project three kinds of transparencies
  Justification: You must work with the projector yourself in order to understand its operation and gain confidence in using it.
2. To evaluate six transparencies you have selected, by completing an evaluation form for each one *(terminal objective)*
  a. To develop a rating scale for evaluating transparencies
  b. To use at least three sources in selecting your transparencies
  Justification: You will probably use many transparencies in your teaching. Therefore, you need a basis for judging their suitability and quality. This procedure will also help you establish a standard of quality for transparencies that you prepare for yourself.
3. To prepare three types of transparencies that, when projected, receive a rating of at least "good" from members of your class.
  a. To make a transparency on acetate with felt pen.
  b. To make a transparency using the thermal process.
  c. To make a transparency using the diazo process.
  Justification: You will need to learn to make your own transparencies because some subject content can be best presented that way.
	Operating the Overhead Projector
	1. Place machine at front of classroom, and stand beside it facing the class.
	2. Controls: (a) on/off fan switch, (b) focus knob, (c) image-elevation knob
	Types of transparencies
	1. Showing all content
	2. Disclosing information by unmasking
	3. Adding overlays to base sheet
	Evaluating Commercial Transparencies
	1. Accuracy of content
	2. Makes good use of overhead features
	3. Technical quality: (a) artwork, (b) lettering size and style, (c) use of color
	Sources of Transparencies
	1. Library file
	2. Department collection
	3. Commercial catalogs
	4. National Information Center for Educational Media (NICEM) reference
	Preparing Transparencies
	1. Felt pens on acetate
	2. Thermal film process: (a) carbon-based original, (b) infrared machine, (c) pass film and original through machine
	3. Diazo film process: (a) opaque drawing on translucent paper, (b) expose drawing and film in ultraviolet light printer, (c) develop film in container of ammonia fumes.

PRE-ASSESSMENT	ACTIVITIES AND RESOURCES

Student Activities

Objective 1

1. Have you used the overhead projector for instructional purposes? (If you answer is yes, reply to Questions 2 and 3.)
2. Describe briefly how extensive your experience has been.
3. How would you rate your ability to use the projector? (If you have had extensive, satisfactory experience with the projector, see your discussion group instructor for permission to skip laboratory practice with the projector.)
4. Have you made your own transparencies for teaching? (If you answer yes, reply to Questions 5 and 6).
5. What techniques have you used?
6. Are any of these transparencies available? (If you feel you are experienced in preparing your own transparencies, discuss with your group instructor the possibility of skipping this part of the topic. You will still be expected to satisfy Objective 3 with transparencies you have already made or with new ones.)

Student Activities

Objective 1

a. Learn how to use the overhead projector by viewing the videotape demonstration, studying the still photographs displayed in the practice laboratory, reading the manual, or any combination of these activities.
b. Complete the worksheet diagram on projector parts and uses.
c. Practice using the projector in the laboratory with sample transparencies.

Objective 2

a. Develop a rating scale for evaluating transparencies.
b. Compare your scale with those on text page 245; revise or add items to yours if you wish.
c. Choose six transparencies and evaluate them; turn in your evaluations to the instructor.

Objective 3

a. Refer to the assignment sheet on making transparencies. Prepare three kinds, and utilize the various techniques as instructed. Make use of 8 mm films and of the procedures printed in the manual. Ask the lab assistant for help if necessary.
b. Sign up with your discussion group to present your transparencies and demonstrate your competence with the projector.
c. Using the rating scale in your manual, you and the instructor will evaluate the transparencies shown by other students in your group.
d. Students who receive unsatisfactory ratings or low scores on a written exercise, use of a projector, or quality of transparencies, review procedures with instructor and repeat any needed laboratory work. Meet again in a group for evaluation.

Instructor Activities

Participate in objectives 2c, 3c, 3d.

EXAMPLE 4. OVERHEAD PROJECTION   147

SUPPORT SERVICES

Budget: $300 for preparing videotape, for preparing still photographs, for purchasing and preparing practice transparencies, for purchasing commercial transparencies and 8 mm films, and for purchasing materials for student production of transparencies.

Personnel: television staff to prepare videotape (3 persons for 8 hours); graphic artist to prepare practice transparencies (12 hours); photographer to prepare display photographs on operation; 2 lab assistants to supervise practice and production lab and assist students (1 week); 2 instructors to meet with ten sections of 20 students each, the following week.

Facilities: equipment laboratory and production laboratory (1 week); resource center (to exhibit commercial transparencies for student inspection); two small-group rooms (10 sections for 40- to 50-minute sessions)

Equipment and Materials: 2 videocassette playback machines and copies of videocassettes on projector operation; 6 overhead projectors in practice laboratory with 25 transparencies for practice; 3 8 mm projectors with 8 mm films on the various production techniques; equipment and supplies for producing transparencies; 200 commercial transparencies for evaluations; printed materials (written exercises); 2 overhead projectors in small-group meeting rooms

EVALUATION

Objective 1: Evaluations are made during presentation by each student in the small-group session.

Objective 2: Evaluations prepared by students are reviewed by the instructor.

Objective 3: Transparencies prepared by students are evaluated in group sessions by other students and the instructor, using the accepted rating scale.

Example 5

GENERAL PURPOSES	STUDENT CHARACTERISTICS
1. To understand that the reason for washing hands is to maintain standards of cleanliness 2. To learn the correct technique for washing hands	60 first-year allied health professional trainees Reading ability, Grades 8–14 Thirty-six students represent cultural minority groups. High level of motivation The previous topic gave background information on microorganisms.

EXAMPLE 5. TECHNIQUE FOR WASHING HANDS   149

LEARNING OBJECTIVES	SUBJECT CONTENT

1. Recognize why washing hands is essential for eliminating microorganisms in health-care work *(terminal objective)*
   Justification: You know the effects of microorganisms, and it is important that you also know the sources of microorganisms, so you can eliminate them.
   a. Name the four routes by which bacteria may be transmitted in a health-care facility.
   b. State at least three circumstances under which you should wash your hands when working in a health-care facility.
2. Demonstrate proper hand-washing technique to two other students and the instructor with 100 percent proficiency *(terminal objective).*
   Justification: You must perform the skill to show your ability.
   a. Wash your hands without any contamination of hands, body, or clothing, performing the six necessary actions and requiring at least two minutes of time.

Routes by Which Bacteria Can Be Transmitted
1. Hospital equipment to patient or worker
2. Patient to patient
3. Worker to worker
4. Worker to patient
5. Patient to worker

Circumstances That Necessitate Washing Hands
1. Before and after contact with a patient
2. After contact with waste or contaminated materials
3. Before handling food or food receptacles
4. Any other time hands become soiled

Technique
1. Turn water on; adjust to warm temperature.
2. Wet hands.
3. Apply soap thoroughly, including under nails and between fingers.
4. Wash palms and backs of hands with ten strong movements.
5. Wash fingers and spaces between them with ten strokes.
6. Wash wrists, and up to three or four inches above the wrists, with ten rotary actions.
7. Repeat Steps 3–6 for the remainder of two minutes.
8. Rinse well, with the final rinse moving from wrist to fingers.
9. Dry thoroughly with a paper towel from wrist to fingers.
10. Turn off water, using a paper towel to cover the faucet, and discard towel.

PRE-ASSESSMENT	ACTIVITIES AND RESOURCES
1. Under which of the following circumstances is it necessary for you to wash your hands? 　a. After contact with a patient 　b. Before handling food 　c. After using a hand lotion 　d. After entering an operating room in surgical dress 2. Name three routes by which bacteria may be transmitted in a hospital. 3. List the steps you feel a hospital employee should take in washing his or her hands correctly.	**Student Activities** 1. Read pages 123–126 in the lab manual. Complete exercise on page 127. 2. View the silent 8 mm film *Handwashing Technique.* 3. Review the pictures and descriptions of the technique in the lab manual (pages 127–130). 4. Practice washing your hands in the laboratory. 5. When ready, demonstrate your ability to wash your hands to two other students. Have them grade you on the scale in the manual (page 131). Discuss their findings and practice your technique again if necessary. 6. When ready, complete the self-check test obtained from the laboratory aide. **Laboratory Aide Activities** 1. Be available to assist students as needed. 2. Test each student on technique.

EXAMPLE 5. TECHNIQUE FOR WASHING HANDS   151

SUPPORT SERVICES	EVALUATION
Budget: $75 for purchase of 3 copies of *Handwashing Technique* 8 mm film Personnel: Laboratory aide to supervise practice; instructor for checkout Facilities: Learning laboratory for 3-day period Equipment and Materials: 4 sinks in laboratory with soap and towels for 60 students, 3 8 mm silent projectors and 3 copies of the film	1. Demonstrate your technique for washing your hands, to your lab aide. 2. Name four routes by which bacteria can be transmitted in a hospital. 3. List three circumstances in a hospital that would necessitate washing your hands.

Bibliography

Many elements of the instructional design plan have been treated in depth elsewhere. This bibliography cites those publications and audiovisual materials that may be most useful if you wish to examine any of them further. Entries appear under the following headings: "Instructional Design Systems," "Learning Objectives," "Learning Theory," "Individualized Learning," "Instructional Resources," "Evaluation," "Equipment," "Facilities," and "Future Planning and Accountability."

Instructional Design Systems

Banathy, Bela H. *Instructional Systems*. Belmont, Calif.: Fearon Publishers, Inc., 1968.

Briggs, Leslie J. *Handbook of Procedures for the Design of Instruction*. Pittsburgh, Pa.: American Institutes for Research, 1970.

Burns, Richard W., and Joe Lars Klingstedt, eds. *Competency-Based Education*. Englewood Cliffs, N.J.: Educational Technology Press, 1972.

Davies, Ivor K. *Competency Based Learning: Technology, Management, and Design*. New York: McGraw-Hill, 1973.

Davis, Robert H.; Lawrence T. Alexander; and Stephen L. Yelon. *Learning System Design: An Approach to the Improvement of Instruction*. New York: McGraw-Hill, 1974.

Diamond, Robert M., and others. *Instructional Development for Individualized Learning in Higher Education*. Englewood Cliffs, N.J.: Educational Technology Publications, 1975.

Drumheller, Sidney J. *Handbook of Curriculum Design for Individualized Instruction*. Englewood Cliffs, N.J.: Educational Technology Publications, 1971.

Eraut, Michael R. "An Instructional Systems Approach to Course Development." *AV Communication Review* Spring 1966, pp. 90–101.

Faris, Gene. "Would You Believe an Instructional Developer?" *Audiovisual Instruction* November 1968, pp. 971–973.

Filbeck, Robert. *Systems in Teaching and Learning*. Lincoln, Nebr.: Professional Education Publications, 1974.

Gagné, Robert M., and Leslie J. Briggs. *Principles of Instructional Design*. New York: Holt, Rinehart and Winston, Inc., 1974.

Gerlach, Vernon S., and Donald P. Ely. *Teaching and Media: A Systems Approach*. Englewood Cliffs, N.J.: Prentice-Hall, 1971.

Gilchrist, Robert S., and Bernice R. Roberts. *Curriculum Development: A Humanized Systems Approach*. Bloomington, Ind.: Phi Delta Kappa, 1974.

Gropper, George L. *Instructional Strategies*. Englewood Cliffs, N.J.: Educational Technology Press, 1974.

Hamreus, Dale G. *The Systems Approach to Instructional Development*. Monmouth, Oreg.: Teaching Research, 1968.

Heinich, Robert. *The Systems Engineering of Education*. Vol. 2, *Applications of Systems Thinking to Instruction*. Los Angeles: Department of Instructional Technology, School of Education, University of Southern California, 1965.

———. *Technology and the Management of Instruction*. Washington, D.C.: Department of Audiovisual Instruction, National Education Association, 1970.

Hoetker, James. *Systems, Systems Approaches, and the Teacher*. Urbana, Ill.: National Council of Teachers of English, 1972.

"Instructional Development: An Emerging Process." *Audiovisual Instruction* December 1971 (entire issue).

Mager, Robert F., and Peter Pipe. *Criterion-Referenced Instruction*. Los Altos Hills, Calif.: Mager Associates, 1974.

———, and Kenneth M. Beach. *Developing Vocational Instruction*. Belmont, Calif.: Fearon Publishers, Inc., 1967.

Merrill, M. David. *Instructional Design: Readings*. Englewood Cliffs, N.J.: Prentice-Hall, 1971.

Popham, W. James. *Criterion-Referenced Instruction*. Belmont, Calif.: Fearon Publishers, Inc., 1974.

———, and Eva K. Baker. *Systematic Instruction*. Englewood Cliffs, N.J.: Prentice-Hall, 1970.

Twelker, Paul A.; Floyd D. Urbach; and James E. Buck. *The Systematic Development of Instruction: An Overview and Basic Guide to the Literature.* Palo Alto, Calif.: ERIC Clearinghouse on Information Resources, Stanford University, 1972.

U.S. Civil Service Commission. *An Application of a Systems Approach to Training: A Case Study.* Washington, D.C.: Bureau of Training, U.S. Civil Service Commission, June 1969.

Wilson, S.R., and D.T. Tosti. *Learning Is Getting Easier.* San Rafael, Calif.: Individual Learning Systems, 1972.

Wong, Martin R., and John D. Raulerson. *A Guide to Systematic Instructional Design.* Englewood Cliffs, N.J.: Educational Technology Publications, 1974.

Learning Objectives

Ammerman, Harry L., and William H. Melching. *The Derivation, Analysis, and Classification of Instructional Objectives.* Alexandria, Va.: Human Resources Research Office, George Washington University, May 1966, technical report 66-4.

Bloom, Benjamin S., and others. *Cognitive Domain.* Taxonomy of Educational Objectives. Handbook 1. New York: David McKay, 1956.

Canfield, Albert A. "A Rationale for Performance Objectives." *Audiovisual Instruction* February 1968, pp. 127–129.

Davies, Ivor K. *Objectives in Curriculum Design.* New York: McGraw-Hill, 1976.

Dillman, Caroline M., and Harold F. Rahmlow. *Writing Instructional Objectives.* Belmont, Calif.: Fearon Publishers, Inc., 1972.

Eiss, Albert F., and Mary B. Blatt. *Behavioral Objectives in the Affective Domain.* Washington, D.C.: National Science Teachers Association, 1969.

Geiss, George L. *Behavioral Objectives: A Selected Bibliography and Brief Review.* Palo Alto, Calif.: ERIC Clearinghouse on Information Resources, Stanford University, 1972.

Gronlund, Norman E. *Stating Behavioral Objectives for Classroom Instruction.* New York: Macmillan, 1970.

Harrow, A.J. *Taxonomy of the Psychomotor Domain.* New York: David McKay, 1972.

Hernandez, David E. *Writing Behavioral Objectives: A Programmed Exercise for Beginners.* New York: Barnes & Noble, 1971.

Kibler, Robert J; Larry L. Barker; and David T. Miles. *Behavioral Objectives and Instruction.* Boston: Allyn & Bacon, 1970.

Koran, John J., Jr.; Ward J. Montague; and Gene E. Hall. *How to Use Behavioral Objectives in Science Instruction.* Washington, D.C.: National Science Teachers Association, 1969.

Krathwohl, David R., and others. *Affective Domain*. Taxonomy of Educational Objectives. Handbook 2. New York: David McKay, 1964.

Kryspin, William J., and John F. Feldhusen. *Writing Behavioral Objectives*. Minneapolis: Burgess, 1974.

Lee, Blaine N., and M. David Merrill. *Writing Complete Affective Objectives: A Short Course*. Belmont, Calif.: Wadsworth, 1972.

Lindvall, C.M., ed. *Defining Educational Objectives*. Pittsburg: University of Pittsburg Press, 1964.

McAshan, H.H. *The Goals Approach to Performance Objectives*. Philadelphia: Saunders, 1974.

Mager, Robert F. *Developing Attitude Toward Learning*. Belmont, Calif.: Fearon Publishers, Inc., 1968.

―――. *Goal Analysis*. Belmont, Calif.: Fearon Publishers, Inc., 1972.

―――. *Preparing Instructional Objectives*. Belmont, Calif.: Fearon Publishers, Inc., 1975.

―――, and Peter Pipe. *Analyzing Performance Problems: Or, You Really Oughta Wanna*. Belmont, Calif.: Fearon Publishers, Inc., 1970.

Mali, Paul. *Managing by Objectives*. New York: Wiley-Interscience, 1972.

Maxwell, John, and Anthony Tovatt. *On Writing Behavioral Objectives for English*. Champaign, Ill.: National Council of Teachers of English, 1970.

National Science Supervisers Association. *Behavioral Objectives in the Affective Domain*. Washington, D.C.: National Science Teachers Association, 1964.

Plowman, Paul D. *Behavioral Objectives: Teacher Success Through Student Performance*. Chicago: Science Research Associates, 1971.

Popham, W. James, and Eva L. Baker. *Establishing Instructional Goals*. Englewood Cliffs, N.J.: Prentice-Hall, 1970.

Poulliotte, Carol A., and Marjorie G. Paters. *Behavioral Objectives: A Comprehensive Bibliography*. Boston: Instructional Technology Information Center, Office of Educational Resources, Northeastern University, 1971.

Vargas, Julie S. *Writing Worthwhile Behavioral Objectives*. New York: Harper & Row, 1972.

Learning Theory

Bloom, Benjamin S. *Learning for Mastery*. Durham, N.C.: Regional Education Laboratory for the Carolinas and Virginia, 1968.

Bugelski, R.B. *The Psychology of Learning Applied to Teaching*. Indianapolis: Bobbs-Merrill, 1971.

Carpenter, Finley, and Eugene E. Hadden. *Systematic Application of Psychology to Education*. New York: Macmillan, 1964.

Gagné, Robert M. *The Conditions of Learning.* New York: Holt, Rinehart and Winston, Inc., 1970.

_____. "Instruction and the Conditions of Learning." In Lawrence Siegel, ed. *Instruction: Some Contemporary Views.* New York: T. Y. Crowell, 1967, pp. 291–316.

_____. "Learning and Communication." In Raymond V. Wiman and Wesley C. Meierhenry, eds. *Educational Media: Theory and Practice.* Columbus, Ohio. Charles E. Merrill, 1969, pp. 93–114.

_____, ed. *Psychological Principles in Systems Development.* New York: Holt, Rinehart and Winston, 1962.

Glaser, Robert. "Psychological Bases for Instructional Design." *AV Communication Review,* Winter 1966, pp. 433–449.

_____, "Toward a Behavioral Science Base for Instructional Design." In Robert Glaser, ed., *Teaching Machines and Programmed Learning.* Vol. 2, *Data and Directions.* Washington, D.C.: National Education Association, 1965, pp. 711–809.

Hill, Joseph E., and Derek N. Nunney. *Personalizing Educational Programs: Utilizing Cognitive Style Mapping.* Bloomfield Hills, Mich.: Oakland Community College.

Homme, Lloyd. *How to Use Contingency Contracting in the Classroom.* Champaign, Ill.: Research Press Co., 1970.

National Special Media Institute. *Contributions of Behavioral Science to Instructional Technology.* Vol. 1, *The Affective Domain;* Vol. 2, *The Cognitive Domain;* Vol. 3, *The Psychomotor Domain.* Washington, D.C.: Gryphon House, 1972.

Tosti, Donald, and John Ball. *A Behavioral Approach to Instructional Design and Media Selection.* Albuquerque, N.Mex.: Behavioral Systems Division, Westinghouse Learning Corporation, 1969.

Individualized Learning

Audio-Tutorial Systems (16 mm sound, color motion picture, 25 minutes). Lafayette, Ind.: Audio-Visual Center, Purdue University, 1969.

Bishop, Lloyd K. *Individualized Educational Systems.* New York: Harper & Row, 1971.

Bolvin, John D. "Implications of the Individualization of Instruction for Curriculum and Instructional Design." *Audiovisual Instruction* March 1968, pp. 238–242.

Creager, Joan G., and Darrel L. Murray. *The Use of Modules in College Biology Teaching.* Washington, D.C.: Commission on Undergraduate Education in the Biological Sciences, 1971.

Drumheller, Sidney J. *Handbook of Curriculum Design for Individualized Instruction*. Englewood Cliffs, N.J.: Educational Technology Publications, 1971.

Duane, James E., ed. *Individualized Instruction: Programs and Materials*. Englewood Cliffs, N.J.: Educational Technology Publications, 1973.

Dunn, Rita, and Kenneth Dunn. *Educator's Self-Teaching Guide to Individualized Instructional Programs*. West Nyack, N.Y.: Parker Publishing Co., 1975.

Edling, Jack V. *Individualized Instruction: A Manual for Administrators*. Corvallis, Oreg.: DCE Publications, Oregon State University, 1970.

Esbensen, Thorwald. *Working with Individualized Instruction*. Belmont, Calif.: Fearon Publishers, Inc., 1968.

Flanagan, John. "Functional Education for the Seventies." *Phi Delta Kappan* September 1967, pp. 27–32.

Gronlund, Norman E. *Individualizing Classroom Instruction*. New York: Macmillan, 1974.

Impelliteri, Joseph, and Curtis R. Finch. *Review and Synthesis of Research on Individualizing Instruction in Vocational and Technical Education*. Columbus: ERIC Clearinghouse on Vocational and Technical Education, Ohio State University, 1971.

Johnson, Stuart, and Rita B. Johnson. *Assuring Learning with Self-Instructional Packages*. Raleigh, N.C.: Self-Instructional Packages, Inc. (P.O. Box 2009, 27514), 1973.

_____. *Developing Individualized Instructional Materials*. Palo Alto, Calif.: Westinghouse Learning Corporation, 1970.

Kapfer, Philip G., and Glen F. Ovard. *Preparing and Using Individualized Learning Packages for Ungraded, Continuous Progress Education*. Englewood Cliffs, N.J.: Educational Technology Publications, 1971.

Keller, Fred S. "Goodbye Teacher. . . ." *Journal of Applied Behavioral Analysis* 1968, pp. 79–89.

_____, and J. Gilmour Sherman. *The Keller Plan Handbook*. Menlo Park, Calif.: W.A. Benjamin, 1974.

Langdon, Danny G. *Interactive Instructional Designs for Individualized Learning*. Englewood Cliffs, N.J.: Educational Technology Publications, 1973.

"Learning Packages." *Educational Technology* September 1972 (entire issue).

McNeil, Jan, and James E. Smith. "The Multis at Nova." *Educational Screen and Audiovisual Guide* January 1968, pp. 6–7.

NSPI Newsletter. Washington, D.C.: National Society for Performance and Instruction.

Nunney, Derek N., and Joseph E. Hill. "Personalized Educational Programs." *Audiovisual Instruction* February 1972, pp. 10–15.

One-to-One: A Newsletter of the International Audio-Tutorial Congress. Washington, D.C.: Association for Educational Communications and Technology.

Postlethwait, S.N.; J. Novak; and H. Murray. *The Audio-Tutorial Approach to Learning.* Minneapolis: Burgess Publishing Company, 1972.

PSI Newsletter. Washington, D.C.: Center for Personalized Instruction, Georgetown University.

Russell, James D. *Modular Instruction.* Minneapolis: Burgess Publishing Company, 1974.

Stice, James E. *The Personalized System of Instruction (PSI): The Keller Plan Applied to Engineering Education.* Austin: College of Engineering, University of Texas, 1971.

Weisberger, Robert A. *Developmental Efforts in Individualized Learning.* Itasca, Ill.: F.E. Peacock, 1971.

_____. *Perspectives in Individualized Learning.* Itasca, Ill.: F.E. Peacock, 1971.

_____. *Trends, Issues and Activities in Individualized Learning.* Palo Alto, Calif.: ERIC Clearinghouse on Information Resources, Stanford University, 1972.

Instructional Resources

Baker, Robert L., and Richard E. Schutz. *Instructional Product Development.* New York: D. Van Nostrand, 1971.

Boocock, Sarane S. *Simulation Games in Learning.* Beverly Hills, Calif.: Sage Publications, 1968.

Boucher, Brian G., and others. *Handbook and Catalog of Instructional Media Selection.* Englewood Cliffs, N.J.: Educational Technology Publications, 1973.

Bretz, Rudy. *The Selection of Appropriate Communications Media for Instruction: A Guide for Designers of Air Force Technical Training Programs.* Santa Monica, Calif.: Rand Corporation, 1971.

_____. *A Taxonomy of Communications Media.* Englewood Cliffs, N.J.: Educational Technology Publications, 1971.

Briggs, Leslie J., and others. *Instructional Media: A Procedure for the Design of Multi-Media Instruction.* Pittsburg: American Institutes for Research, 1967.

Brown, James W.; Richard B. Lewis; and Fred F. Harcleroad. *AV Instruction: Technology, Media and Methods.* New York: McGraw-Hill, 1977.

Dale, Edgar. *Audiovisual Methods in Teaching.* New York: Holt, Rinehart and Winston, Inc. 1969.

Dyer, Charles A. *Preparing for Computer Assisted Instruction.* Englewood Cliffs, N.J.: Educational Technology Publications, 1972.

Kemp, Jerrold E. *Planning and Producing Audiovisual Materials.* New York: T. Y. Crowell, 1975.

Lawson, Tom E. *Formative Instructional Product Evaluation: Instruments and Strategies.* Englewood Cliffs, N.J.: Educational Technology Publications, 1974.

Merrill, M. David, and R. Irwin Goodman. *Selecting Instructional Strategies and Media.* Washington, D.C.: National Special Media Institutes, 1972.

Stadsklev, Ron. *Handbook of Simulation Gaming in Social Education.* Huntsville: Institute of Higher Education Research, University of Alabama, 1975.

Wittich, Walter, and Charles Schuller. *Instructional Technology: Its Nature and Use.* New York: Harper & Row, 1973.

Zuckerman, David W., and Robert E. Horn. *The Guide to Simulations/Games for Education and Training.* Hicksville, N.Y.: Research Media, Inc., 1973.

Evaluation

Block, James H. *Mastery Learning: Theory and Practice.* New York: Holt, Rinehart and Winston, Inc., 1971.

Bloom, Benjamin S., and others. *Handbook on Formative and Summative Evaluation of Student Learning.* New York: McGraw-Hill, 1971.

Dressel, Paul, and Clarence Nelson. *Questions and Problems in Science,* test folio 1. Princeton, N.J.: Educational Testing Service, 1956.

Eisner, Elliot W. "Emerging Models for Educational Evaluation." *School Review,* August 1972, pp. 573–589.

Gronlund, Normal E. *Measurement and Evaluation in Teaching.* New York: Macmillan, 1971.

_____. *Preparing Criterion-Referenced Tests for Classroom Instruction.* New York: Macmillan, 1973.

Kryspin, William J., and John F. Feldhusen. *Developing Classroom Tests.* Minneapolis: Burgess Publishing Company, 1974.

Lippey, Gerald. *Computer-Assisted Test Construction.* Englewood Cliffs, N.J.: Educational Technology Publications, 1974.

Mager, Robert F. *Measuring Instructional Intent.* Belmont, Calif.: Fearon Publishers, Inc., 1973.

Nagel, Thomas S., and Paul T. Richman. *Competency-Based Instruction.* Columbus, Ohio: Charles E. Merrill, 1972.

Popham, W. James. *Criterion-Referenced Measurement.* Englewood Cliffs, N.J.: Educational Technology Publications, 1971.

Sanders, Norris M. *Classroom Questions: What Kinds?* New York: Harper & Row, 1966.

Testing and Evaluation in the Biological Sciences. Washington, D.C.: Commission on Undergraduate Education in the Biological Sciences, 1967.

Equipment

The Audio-Visual Equipment Directory. Fairfax, Va.: National Audio-Visual Association (annual).

Facilities

Church, John. *Administration of Instructional Materials Organizations.* Belmont, Calif.: Fearon Publishers, Inc., 1970.

DeBernardis, Amo, and others. *Planning Schools for New Media.* Portland, Oreg.: Division of Education, Portland State College, 1961.

Green, Alan C., ed. *Educational Facilities with New Media.* Washington, D.C.: National Education Association, 1966.

Gunselman, Marshall. *What Are We Hearing About Learning Centers?* Oklahoma City: Eagle Media, Oklahoma Christian College, 1971.

Mahar, Mary H., ed. *The School Library as a Materials Center.* Washington, D.C.: U.S. Office of Education, 1964.

New Arrangements for Learning: The Media-Facilities Story (35 mm sound-color filmstrip, 90 frames/18 minutes). Seattle: University of Washington, 1967.

Space Is Not Enough: Planning Facilities for Media (35 mm sound-color filmstrip, 86 frames/22 minutes). Fairfax, Va.: National Audio-Visual Association, 1968.

The School Library: Facilities for Independent Study in the Secondary School (1963) and *Study Carrels: Designs for Independent Study Space* (1964). New York: Educational Facilities Laboratories (455 Madison Avenue 10022). (Other publications on facilities are also available.)

Teachey, William G., and Joseph B. Carter. *Learning Laboratories: A Guide to Adoption and Use.* Englewood Cliffs, N.J.: Educational Technology Publications, 1971.

Future Planning and Accountability

Carnegie Commission on Higher Education. *The Fourth Revolution: Instructional Technology in Higher Education.* New York: McGraw-Hill, 1972.

Center for Improvement of Undergraduate Education, Cornell University. *The Yellow Pages of Undergraduate Innovations.* New Rochelle, N.Y. *Change* Magazine, 1974.

Dietrich, John E., and F. Craig Johnson. "A Catalytic Agent for Innovation in Higher Education." *Educational Record* Summer 1967, pp. 206–213.

Hack, Walter G., and others. *Educational Futurism, 1985.* Berkeley, Calif.: McCutchan Publishing Corporation, 1971.

Haney, John; Phil Lange; and John Barson. "The Heuristic Dimension of Instructional Development." *AV Communication Review* Winter 1968, pp. 358–371.

Harmon, Paul. "Curriculum Cost-Effectiveness Evaluation." *Audiovisual Instruction* January 1970, pp. 24–26, 76–77.

Hartley, Harry J. *Educational Planning—Programming—Budgeting.* Englewood Cliffs, N.J.: Prentice-Hall, 1968.

Humphrey, David A. *Instructional Development: The Problems of Costs and Effectiveness.* ERIC document no. ED-092-045, March 12, 1974. Available from ERIC Document Reproduction Service, P.O. Box 190, Arlington, Va. 22210

Lessinger, Leon, and Ralph W. Tyler. *Accountability in Education.* Worthington, Ohio: Charles A. Jones, 1971.

McBeath, Ron J. "Is Education Becoming?" *AV Communication Review* Spring 1969, pp. 36–40.

————. "Program Planning and Management in Audiovisual Services." *Audiovisual Instruction* October 1971, pp. 62–67.

Nance, John B. "Operations Research Analysis of Audio-Tutorial Systems," *Educational Technology* June 1973, pp. 64–72.

Shane, Harold G. *The Educational Significance of the Future.* Bloomington, Ind.: Phi Delta Kappa, 1973.

Spangenberg, Ronald W.; Riback, Vair; and Moon, Harold L. *The State of Knowledge Pertaining to Selection of Cost-Effective Training Methods and Media.* Alexandria, Va.: Human Resources Research Organization, June 1973.

Tickton, Sidney G., ed. *To Improve Learning: An Evaluation of Instructional Technology.* New York: R.R. Bowker, 1970.

Wilkinson, Gene L. "Cost Evaluation of Instructional Strategies." *AV Communication Review* spring 1973, pp. 11–29.

DATE DUE

6. 10. '82	
10. 14 '82	
10. 25. '84	
Due UCC 11/09/84	
12. 07 '85	
2. 21 '85	
MAR 1 8 2002	